PRAISE FOR
PRODUCING A BLOCKBUSTER BUSINESS

"I loved the book and its unique approach to understanding leadership. *Producing a Blockbuster Business* draws out the hidden stories of leadership that are imbedded in some of our favorite movies. It helps us understand how the leaders on the screen apply sound principles that we can all use to make us better leaders, both at home and at work."

— David Booth, Founder and Chairman, Dimensional Fund Advisors; and Namesake of the University of Chicago Booth School of Business

"'You talking to me?' asks Travis Bickle in *Taxi Driver*. Well, if you are interested in learning important leadership principles presented in a succinct memorable way, then David Wescoe is talking to you."

— Perry Golkin, CEO & Founder, PPC Enterprises; former General Partner, KKR; and Trustee Emeritus, University of Pennsylvania

"An easy and entertaining read. The leadership lessons will stay with you long after the final credits roll."

"David uses recognizable scenes from films to illustrate important leadership principles. The book's insights, thoughtful content, and humor will keep you turning the pages."

"David's blend of wisdom from the world of business and films is unique. As an executive leadership coach and movie producer, I know that the leadership lessons in *Producing a Blockbuster Business* are what make a film—or an organization—great. The book's insights provide a clear sense of what it takes to 'make it,' as is often said in the film industry. You would be wise to read, understand, and apply these lessons."

"I was practically born in a movie theater, and I have been watching movies ever since. *Producing a Blockbuster Business* uses many of my favorite films to teach important leadership lessons. Grab some popcorn and read this book."

—*Eli Durst, award-winning photographer; author; and Guggenheim Fellow*

PRODUCING A BLOCKBUSTER BUSINESS

PRODUCING A BLOCKBUSTER BUSINESS

Ten Leadership Lessons from the Movies

David Wescoe
Anthony Picchioni, PhD

Illustrations by Elliot Lang

Producing a Blockbuster Business

Editor: Eric Hübler, erichublerediting. com
Cover designer: Pagatana Design Service
Interior Designer: Amit Dey, amitdey2528@gmail.com
Publishing Consultant: Geoff Affleck, AuthorPreneur Publishing Inc., authorpreneurbooks.com

ISBN 979-8-9937221-0-8 (paperback)
ISBN 979-8-9937221-1-5 (ebook)
ISBN 979-8-9937221-2-2 (audiobook)

The profits from the sales of *Producing a Blockbuster Business* will be donated to the Motion Picture & Television Fund in Woodland Hills, CA.

We did not write this volume for a commercial purpose or pecuniary gain.

Rather, we wrote it because of our love of movies, our respect for the people who make them, and our interest in using cinema leadership lessons to help readers become better leaders.

Therefore, it is our privilege to donate the profits from the sales of *Producing a Blockbuster Business* to the Motion Picture & Television Fund in Woodland Hills, CA. For more than a century, the MPTF has fulfilled its mission to support "the entertainment community in living and aging well, with dignity and purpose, and in helping each other in times of need."

For more information about or to donate to MPTF, please visit mptf.com.

David & Tony

Contents

Foreword

"Find something in your purse, briefcase, wallet, or wherever you carry meaningful mementos that represents something you value in your life. Take it out and explain to the group what it is, what it means, and why you carry it with you."

I use this icebreaker when I facilitate leader groups and discuss what it takes to build strong, heart-led teams to successfully run their organizations.

In my first meeting with David Wescoe, he opened his wallet and shared a picture with the group: "This is a picture of one of my sons, who has struggled with some life decisions and issues, and I hope I have done my best to be a good father, support, and role model in his life."

Then the tears began. Not just David's, but everyone else in the room, too. We were all touched by David's sincerity, openness, and emotion.

Every now and then, a special person walks into a room, and your life, and lights it up with wisdom, humor, and likeability. Reading *Producing a Blockbuster Business* is all the evidence you will need to know that David is that guy. David's blend of wisdom from the world of business and films is unique. As an executive leadership coach and movie producer, I know that the leadership lessons in *Producing a Blockbuster Business* are what make a film—or an organization—great. The book's insights provide a clear sense of what it takes to "make it," as is often said in the film industry. You would be wise to read, understand, and apply these principles.

– Steve Alexander, movie producer;
Founding Partner, AHA Productions;
and executive leadership coach

PREFACE

Why, you ask, would someone write—or read—another business book?

There are dozens of popular and academic articles and books published every year about leadership. What can I possibly say that hasn't already been said by other authors, academics, or business executives? What could I add to the voluminous literature about leadership?

One of this book's themes is that leaders ask "Why?" (like Humphrey Bogart's Rick Blaine in *Casablanca* who asks himself why, of all the gin joints in all the towns in all the world, did his long-lost love Ilsa Lund have to walk into his). So, when I thought about writing this book, I asked myself, "Why?"

Well, here's why.

Management guru Tom Peters has said, "The best leaders . . . almost without exception and at every level, are master users of stories and symbols." I love movies. (I was the chief executive of the Motion Picture Industry Pension and Health Plans for a time.) And many movies have stories and scenes that emphasize important leadership principles.

Indeed, I am often teased about managing by screenplay. During meetings or in conversations with colleagues, I'll often ask, "What movie does that remind me of?" or refer to a movie scene to make a point.

Even with algorithms and artificial intelligence, most work gets done by real people. And in my experience, co-workers are more effective if they follow simple and time-tested management principles. If a leader can articulate these principles in an entertaining and accessible way using stories and symbols, it is more likely that their colleagues will remember and apply them. I wrote this book to share some of my favorite movie moments that illustrate important management principles and leadership lessons.

A few of the movies I discuss, like *The Wizard of Oz* and *It's a Wonderful Life*, are older than I am. And some of the films I discuss might be ones you haven't seen (my advice: Stream them!), but their leadership lessons are timeless and will make you a better leader.

Finally, I am fortunate that my good friend and distinguished professional counselor, Dr. Anthony Picchioni, who has decades of organizational and management consulting and executive coaching experience with Fortune 500 companies around the world, agreed to join me in this endeavor. His insights improved it.

– David Wescoe, January 2026

CHAPTER ONE

CREATE IT: ARTICULATE A CLEAR VISION

The difference between a mediocre movie and a blockbuster often depends on the director's vision. Directors craft unforgettable films by translating their vision to the screen and by inspiring their cast and crew to bring their vision to life.

Like a director, a leader needs to articulate a vision effectively so that colleagues and stakeholders understand and are inspired by it. Then, the leader must translate that vision into organizational success.

Organizations and the environments in which they operate are complex. Leaders must recast this complexity into a simple, but powerful, vision that resonates with diverse audiences.

1

By creating a compelling narrative, a leader will create a deep sense of purpose, even urgency, that will drive their organization to success.

Great leaders are often dreamers. They can take an idea and turn it into a remarkable reality. To paraphrase George Bernard Shaw, while most may see things as they are and say "Why?" leaders dream of things that never were and say, "Why not?"

Many movie characters have vision, and I will discuss a few of my favorites in this chapter.

Field of Dreams is an inspiring movie where a character's dream becomes a vision realized. The movie was based on the book *Shoeless Joe* by W. P. Kinsella and was written and directed by Phil Alden Robinson (*Sneakers* and *Sum of All Fears*). It was nominated for three Academy

Awards, including Best Picture, and has been selected for preservation in the United States National Film Registry by the Library of Congress for being "culturally, historically, or aesthetically significant." James Earl Jones has a terrific role, as does Burt Lancaster in his final film role.

The movie tells the story of Iowa farmer Ray Kinsella (Kevin Costner) who, while walking in his cornfield one evening, sees a vision of the field turned into a baseball diamond with the ghost of baseball legend Shoeless Joe Jackson (Ray Liotta) standing on it. He hears a voice that tells him, "If you build it, he will come" (No. 39 on the American Film Institute's 100 Greatest Movie Quotes of All Time). Kinsella acts on his vision, and if you ever find yourself on the road near Dyersville, Iowa, you can stop by the Field of Dreams Movie Site ("The Most Magical Place on Dirt!") from sunrise to sunset year-round and walk on the field and dream yourself.

The most effective visions are also inspirational. For a vision that inspires, it's tough to beat ***It's a Wonderful Life***. Directed by the legendary director Frank Capra, the American Film Institute ranks *It's a Wonderful Life* No. 1 on its 100 Most Inspiring Films of All Time list. But the movie didn't have much success at the Academy Awards. Although it was nominated for five Oscars, including Best Motion Picture, Directing, and Best Actor, it didn't win any. The big winner was *The Best Years of Our Lives*, which was nominated for eight Oscars and won seven, including Best Motion Picture. Fredric

March, who starred a few years later in *Executive Suite*, won the Oscar for Best Actor.

It's a Wonderful Life stars Jimmy Stewart as George Bailey who has big, but unfulfilled, dreams. George lives in the small upstate New York town of Bedford Falls running Bailey Building and Loan, which was founded by his father, along with George's bumbling Uncle Billy.

George's father had an inspiring vision for the Building and Loan: He believed that the business was doing something important by providing home loans to lower-and middle-class borrowers. But because of that altruistic vision, the Bailey Building and Loan is a thorn in the side of the greedy Bedford Falls businessman Henry Potter (Lionel Barrymore), who wants to put it out of business.

Potter gets his chance when Uncle Billy loses a bank deposit, and a bank examiner finds the discrepancy in the bank's books on the day before Christmas. George is forced to ask Potter for a loan, but Potter gleefully refuses.

Driven to despair, George is ready to end his life by jumping off a bridge. But just before he takes his leap, Angel Second Class Clarence Odbody, who is sent to earth as George's guardian angel, magically appears. When George tells Clarence that he wished that he'd never been born, Clarence shows George what Bedford Falls would have become if he hadn't been born. It is not a pretty picture.

With no George, Bedford Falls is no more; it's now Pottersville, a dreary community full of bars and sleazy nightclubs. George's house is now abandoned, and his wife and children never were. Uncle Billy is in an insane asylum. After showing this grim scenario to George, Clarence's message is that George really had a wonderful life.

Convinced by Clarence's tour of Pottersville, George doesn't jump. Instead, when the Bailey Building and

Loan's depositors learn of its troubles, they come together to save it. The movie ends with bells ringing (announcing that Clarence finally got his angel's wings), and George celebrating with family and friends. A powerful lesson in leadership.

The movie's story makes an important point about visions: The most powerful are inspiring, too. George's father's vision for The Bailey Building and Loan wasn't just to make loans; it was to help working people become financially independent homeowners. Jimmy Stewart's George Bailey transformed his father's vision and turned indifferent individuals into a powerful collective. Much like a credit union, the Building and Loan was less about profit and more about helping its customers succeed. Just as Frank Capra brought George's story to life, the most effective leaders articulate an inspiring vision and align their colleagues and customers around that vision to motivate purposeful action.

Since I left private law practice, I have been fortunate to work for organizations with inspiring visions that touch people's lives, most recently as a public servant managing public retirement systems. My message to colleagues was simple: You are fortunate to work for an organization that is in a life-touching business. Hundreds of thousands of public employees depend on us for their financial security in retirement.

No matter what the organization's product or service, the leader who can create a vision that includes a sense of meaningful purpose that improves its customers' lives will be on their way to success.

Sometimes, however, there isn't just one visionary leading the way. Organizations can have powerful constituencies with competing visions for the future. Business literature is littered with boardroom battles among directors, executives, shareholders, and stakeholders, each arguing about an organization's vision, including succession, ethics, employee engagement, and the trade-off between profits and product quality.

A few years back, Facebook's chief information security officer left the company over internal disagreements about how much Facebook should publicly disclose about nation-states using the platform to impact the 2016 U.S. elections. The departing executive had pushed for more disclosure but was overruled. Commenting on the departure in *The New York Times*, one former Facebook employee said, "The people whose job it is to protect the user always are fighting an uphill battle against the people whose job it is to make money for the company." A cybersecurity consultant added, "You can eat well or sleep well, but seldom both."

Executive Suite is a terrific movie that depicts a boardroom battle between two powerful, but competing, organizational visions. Deciding which vision will prevail will define the company's soul.

One of the most amazing things about this movie is that although it was released more than seven decades ago, the leadership and vision struggles it portrays are even more relevant today.

Based on Cameron Hawley's 1952 novel of the same name, *Executive Suite* focuses on the struggle for control of the Tredway Corporation, a large furniture manufacturer, after the unexpected death of its CEO, Avery Bullard. Directed by Robert Wise with the screenplay written by Ernest Lehman, the movie is filmed in black and white without a musical score. Nominated for four Oscars, the cast included four Oscar winners (William Holden, Fredric March, Dean Jagger, and Shelley Winters), and four Oscar nominees (Barbara Stanwyck, Walter Pidgeon, Nina Foch, and Louis Calhern).

After Bullard drops dead on a city sidewalk, Tredway's board of directors meets to choose his successor. In a dramatic boardroom meeting, the board must decide between two starkly different visions for the company. Loren Shaw (Fredric March), the company's controller, focuses his vision solely on financial measures, putting increasing earnings and dividends above all else. The company's idealistic product development executive, McDonald Walling (William Holden), passionately argues for an alternative vision: That it's in the company's best interest to produce high-quality products that employees will be proud to build for a brand that customers can trust. If the company does this, then financial success will follow.

After the two executives finish articulating their visions for the company, the board unanimously elects Walling

CEO. The board makes that choice because while many may have a vision, effective leaders have the ability, like Walling, to inspire others to embrace it. Only then does a vision become reality.

One of my favorite visions is the four-legged star in *Seabiscuit.* Based on Laura Hillenbrand's 2001 bestseller, *Seabiscuit: An American Legend*, the film was nominated for seven Academy Awards, including Best Picture. While the movie didn't win any Oscars, it sold more than five million DVDs, the most ever for a dramatic movie at the time.

In addition to the horse, *Seabiscuit* focuses on three other characters, each of whom overcomes personal challenges through their relationship with Seabiscuit and each other. Charles Howard (Jeff Bridges) is a successful car dealer and one of the richest men in California. He lost his son in a car crash and his wife in divorce. Tom Smith (Chris Cooper) is a horse-loving drifter. Red Pollard (Tobey Maguire) is a talented jockey with a love of literature.

Tom discovers Seabiscuit and convinces Charles to buy the horse. Then they hire Red to be Seabiscuit's jockey. As Seabiscuit's legend grows (in 1938, Seabiscuit reportedly received more newspaper coverage than Roosevelt, Hitler, or Mussolini), Charles challenges Samuel Riddle, who owns Triple Crown winner War Admiral, to a race between Seabiscuit and War Admiral. Riddle agrees but insists that the race be held at Pimlico, War Admiral's home track in Baltimore.

At Pimlico, in one of the decade's biggest sporting events, Seabiscuit pulls away in the home stretch and beats War Admiral by four lengths.

To me, *Seabiscuit* beautifully expresses a vision of success.

With the movie as my inspiration, one of the most successful visions that I ever created was another horse: Nyquist. I'd never heard of Nyquist until I woke up the first Sunday morning in May of 2016, opened the paper,

and read that Nyquist had won the Kentucky Derby. But what really caught my eye was Nyquist's front-page picture leading the field down the backstretch, his coat clean and glistening. Every other horse in the field was behind him, muddy and miserable on the wet track. Nyquist was an inspiring sight.

Looking at that image of Nyquist, who was headed for the winner's circle, I saw a powerful vision. Doesn't every leader want their organization, no matter its product or service, to be the leader with the competition in the dust (or mud) behind them?

On Monday, I assembled my leadership team and showed them the Nyquist photo. I said, "This is my vision: Be Nyquist." Our business didn't matter (it happened to be a public pension plan); our vision was simply to be the best at what we do.

It worked. Nyquist created a vivid image of success. Employees got it and remembered it. Soon, many of them had pictures of Nyquist on their desks. And, leveraging the Nyquist theme, we began giving employees horseshoes to recognize outstanding performance. It was an inspiring vision, and I have used it ever since.

CHAPTER TWO

SCRIPT IT: THINK STRATEGICALLY

Spoiler alert: A leader can articulate a clear and inspiring vision, but without effective strategies to achieve it, it will never be more than a vision. If vision is the *what* of successful leadership, strategy is the *how*. While the vision sets the scene, strategies determine how to film it.

Strategic thinking is essential for leaders in any sector (public, private, or nonprofit), whether they're striving to differentiate their organization in a competitive commercial marketplace or navigating the complexities of allocating public resources.

Harvard Business School Professor Michael Porter teaches us that an organization's strategy helps it identify its competitive advantages, those unique attributes and capabilities that allow it to outperform its competitors.

Strategy defines the markets the organization should enter (or exit) and the products and services it should (or shouldn't) offer its customers. Strategy focuses on how to allocate the organization's finite resources (capital, personnel, and technology) to ensure that the right resources are available in the right places at the right times. Strategy identifies internal (organic) and external (acquisitive) growth opportunities. Strategy can blunt competitive threats and help organizations respond to changing market conditions.

But even when a leader thinks they have implemented effective and successful strategies, it is important that they remember the observation often attributed to Winston Churchill: "However beautiful the strategy, you should occasionally look at the results."

Leaders should frequently evaluate their strategies and be flexible enough to change them if circumstances change—which they inevitably will.

Whenever I began to feel too comfortable about my current strategies, I reminded myself about my commute when I worked in Los Angeles. Every Monday, I rode Amtrak's Pacific Surfliner from San Diego to LA, and every Friday I rode it back home to San Diego. As the train pulled into LA's Union Station, it passed a sad and depressing sight: a colossal, abandoned building that once had been part of a thriving commercial enterprise. But now the building was empty, tagged with graffiti, its windows broken or boarded up. But on the building's top floor, I could still make out the faded name of its owner, "Sears, Roebuck and Company."

The movie characters in this chapter didn't know it, but each was following Professor Porter's theories as they implemented successful strategies for their organizations.

Moneyball was based on Michael Lewis's bestselling book, *Moneyball: The Art of Winning an Unfair Game*. It was directed by Bennett Miller (*Capote* and *Foxcatcher*) with the screenplay written by Aaron Sorkin (*A Few Good Men, The American President,* and *The West Wing*) and Steven Zaillian (*Searching for Bobby Fischer, A Civil Action,* and *The Irishman*). It was nominated for six Academy Awards, including Best Picture, Actors in Leading and Supporting Roles (Brad Pitt and Jonah Hill), and Writing (Adapted Screenplay). It was the third baseball movie to be nominated for Best Picture after *Pride of the Yankees* and *Field of Dreams*.

The Oakland Athletics are a low-budget Major League Baseball franchise in a small-market town. *Moneyball* tells the true story of how Billy Beane, the A's general manager, turned one of the poorest franchises in baseball into a World Series contender. And he does it by ignoring many of the game's most treasured strategies.

Because Beane (Brad Pitt, "giving the quintessential Brad Pitt performance") knows that the A's will never have

the player payroll to compete with wealthier teams in larger markets, he hired the pseudonymous Peter Brand (Jonah Hill), a recent Yale economics major, to help construct a roster the A's could afford by finding undervalued (i.e., cheaper) players.

Beane and Brand rejected many of baseball's longest-held truisms and instead implemented Bill James's theories of baseball analytics. James is a distinguished resident of Lawrence, Kansas, who, while working as a night watchman at a Stokley-Van Camp plant, developed new statistical analytics that revolutionized baseball strategy. James's work caught the eye of the Boston Red Sox, who hired him as a senior adviser and went on to win several World Series championships using his analytics.

Beane and Brand were James disciples and used his analytical models to find players other Major League teams didn't want but whose statistics showed they could get on base or get batters out. Most importantly, they were players the A's could afford.

The strategy was unorthodox, but because of the A's fragile financial position, it had to be. Old-school baseball guys, like A's manager Art Howe (Philip Seymour Hoffman) and other baseball traditionalists, hated the new analytical, numbers-focused player evaluation process. But Beane and Brant stick with their strategy, and, in 2002, the A's were one of the most exciting teams in baseball history, winning 103 games, including an American League record twenty consecutive games.

Outspent by millions (the Yankees' payroll was $114 million; the A's was $39 million), Beane and Brand put together a team that included the American League's MVP (Miguel Tejada) and Cy Young Award winner (Barry Zito). The strategy was successful because Beane and Brand found hitters who got on base and pitchers who got opposing hitters out. Simplicity itself.

Just like every Major League Baseball team can't have the payroll the Yankees and Dodgers do, not everyone can (or wants) to work for an established name-brand firm or exciting, well-funded start-up. There are a million Oakland A's organizations. The challenge, then, as Professor Porter writes, is to "achieve sustainable competitive advantage by preserving what is distinctive about a company. It means performing *different* activities from rivals, or performing *similar* activities in different ways." Just like the A's.

As leaders develop and implement their organization's strategies, it is just as important that they keep an eye on their competitors' strategies. John le Carré's George Smiley, the second most famous British spy, knew that if MI6 wanted to be ahead of the game, it had to guess where the game would go. (Neither Alec Guinness's nor Gary Oldman's portrayals of George Smiley in their film versions of *Tinker Tailor Soldier Spy* should be missed.)

And while anticipating what the competition will do, some leaders focus instead on territory where no one has ever been. Steve Jobs famously said,

> Some people say, "Give the customers what they want." But that's not my approach. Our job is to figure out what they're going to want before they do. I think Henry Ford once said, "If I'd asked customers what they wanted, they would have told me, 'A faster horse!'" People don't know what they want until you show it to them. That's why I never rely on market research. Our task is to read things that are not yet on the page.

One movie character who dramatically succeeds by anticipating his competition (which happened to be the German army) is General George Patton (George C. Scott), one of the most successful and controversial combat commanders in U.S. history.

Patton, directed by Franklin Schaffner (*Planet of the Apes*, *Papillon*, and *The Boys from Brazil*) and written by, among others, Francis Ford Coppola, was nominated for ten Academy Awards and won seven, including Best Picture and Directing. Scott won the Oscar for Best Actor, but he refused to accept it because he didn't believe in competition among actors.

The movie begins with a dramatic scene of Patton addressing his troops (and the audience) while standing in front of a massive U.S. flag. Among his many inspirational words, Patton reminds his troops that no one ever won a war by dying for his country; men win wars by making the enemy's soldiers die for theirs.

In December 1944, Europe is suffering through one of its worst winters in history. Allied forces are hunkered down, and their commanders assume the Germans are, too. But not Patton. In one scene, Patton is pacing in his room at night thinking out loud to himself. In his analysis, there is no reason to assume the Germans would mount a major offensive: The weather is awful, the Germans' supplies are low, and the German army hasn't mounted a winter offensive since Frederick the Great. Given these facts, what does Patton conclude? That the Germans will indeed attack.

Patton is right. Hitler launches a massive counteroffensive, the Battle of the Bulge, the bloodiest battle of the war. Caught off guard, senior Allied commanders meet at Verdun to decide what to do. Their most pressing concern is that the Germans have the Army's 101st Airborne Division trapped at Bastogne.

Relieving the 101st Airborne is critical to Allied success, and General Eisenhower wants to know who can do it. After the British say they can't, Patton responds that his staff is already working out the details, and he can attack with three divisions in forty-eight hours.

Patton's prescience pays off. A few weeks later, in a movie theater newsreel, Americans heard Lowell Thomas report that Patton's Third Army had relieved Bastogne and the 18,000 U.S. troops trapped there on the day after Christmas. In doing so, Patton's Third Army moved farther and faster, and engaged more divisions in less time, than any other army in U.S. history.

Another critical aspect of a leader's strategy is knowing what the organization won't do. As Professor Porter reminds us, "Strategy requires you to make trade-offs in competing—to choose what *not* to do."

A scene from **The Godfather** proves Porter's point—and it's probably not the scene you're thinking of. Based on Mario Puzo's blockbuster novel and directed by Francis Ford Coppola, *The Godfather* was nominated for ten Oscars and won three: Best Picture, Best Actor (Marlon Brando), and Writing (Screenplay based on material from another

medium: Puzo and Coppola). Like George C. Scott, who won for *Patton*, Brando, who won the Oscar for portraying Don Vito Corleone, aka The Godfather, refused to accept the award. Al Pacino, who was nominated for Actor in a Supporting Role, would be nominated for an Academy

Award the next three years for his roles in *Serpico*, *The Godfather Part II*, and *Dog Day Afternoon*.

The movie opens in New York in the summer of 1945, where the Godfather is hosting a wedding reception at his estate for his daughter Connie (Talia Shire) and her husband Carlo Rizzi (Gianni Russo). During the reception, many of the guests meet privately with the Godfather because, as the Godfather's consigliere Tom Hagen (Robert Duvall) explains, no Sicilian can refuse a request on his daughter's wedding day.

One guest who visits the Godfather is his godson, singer Johnny Fontane (Al Martino). Johnny asks the Godfather to help him convince a Hollywood movie producer to cast him in his upcoming movie. Johnny is convinced the role will get his career back on track. The Godfather agrees to help: "I'm gonna make him an offer he can't refuse" (No. 2 on AFI's 100 Greatest Movie Quotes). However, the producer (played by John Marley) does refuse the Godfather's offer. Big mistake. He soon reverses himself after receiving a terrifying revised offer. Johnny gets the part.

A bit later in the movie, the Godfather makes a fateful strategic decision *not* to do something, and this is where we see Porter's wisdom illustrated. He meets with an ambitious drug dealer allied with a rival crime family who is seeking to partner with him in distributing narcotics.

Despite the potential for significant profits and against the advice of his closest advisors, the Godfather rejects the proposal. His reasoning is simple: Narcotics is a high-risk

business, much more so than gambling and prostitution. The Godfather evaluates the options and decides that the politicians and judges who protect his business interests would stop doing so if narcotics were involved.

The Godfather's strategic decision not to get involved in the drug business has severe consequences for his family and its business, which plays out in grizzly detail in the movie.

After the Godfather's (natural) death, his son Michael becomes Godfather. Michael moves the family's operations to Nevada, but before leaving New York, he ruthlessly settles all the family's scores.

All this mayhem is the result of the Godfather's refusal to partner in the drug business. In doing so, the Godfather anticipates Professor Porter's advice that an effective strategy is just as important in helping organizations avoid seemingly attractive but ultimately incompatible opportunities, as it is in focusing the organization on opportunities that should be pursued. The Godfather knows that the opportunity for profits in the narcotics business, however enticing, isn't consistent with the family's business strategy. Successful leaders know what their organization's strengths are and leverage them strategically. They avoid opportunities that will undermine their organization's strengths.

PLAN IT: FOCUS ON THE DETAILS

Success—like the proverbial devil—is in the details.

**Leaders don't just focus on the big picture.
They pay attention to the details.**

Colin Powell knew that "success ultimately rests on small things, lots of small things. Leaders have to have a feel for small things—a feel for what is going on in the depths of an organization where small things reside One way is to leave the top floor and its grand accoutrements and get down into the bowels for real. Don't tell anyone you're coming."

In **Casino**, directed by Martin Scorsese (*Taxi Driver, Raging Bull, Goodfellas,* and *The Wolf of Wall Street*), Robert De Niro stars as "Ace" Rothstein, a professional gambler that Midwestern mob families send to Las Vegas to run the mythical Tangiers Casino. Ace runs a smooth operation and significantly increases the casino's profitability. He marries the beautiful Ginger McKenna (Sharon Stone, an Oscar nominee for Actress in a Leading Role) and is soon joined by his good friend Nicky Santoro (Joe Pesci), who is sent to Vegas by the mob ostensibly to protect Ace and the business. Nicky, of course, has other ideas. (With Pesci cast in one of his patented mob roles, it's not surprising that when *Casino* was released it held the record for the most times the F-word was uttered in a movie: 435.)

One reason Ace is so successful running the Tangiers is his attention to the details. In one scene, Ace is having breakfast in the casino's restaurant with Phillip Green (Kevin Pollak), the casino's titular CEO. Ace explains that Green is up on the top floor in his office focused on finances and he can't see what's going on the casino floor. Ace, on the other hand, is on the floor all the time watching all the details. And when Ace is on the floor, there isn't a single thing he doesn't notice.

During this conversation, Ace compares his blueberry muffin with Green's. Ace points out that Green's muffin is full of blueberries, while Ace's has almost none.

Ace is incensed. Finding the situation intolerable, he gets up from the table and walks into the kitchen, with Green in his wake. Ace finds the chef and makes it clear to him that going forward each muffin must have the same number of blueberries in it.

Ace emphasizes that there is no detail that he doesn't notice to ensure that each casino guest will have the same excellent experience and service, including the same number of berries in their muffins. Ace, like all successful leaders, pays close attention to details and drives that behavior throughout the organization. (And now, whenever my granddaughter and I make blueberry muffins, she teases me, "Papa, did I put the same number of blueberries in each muffin?")

It's unlikely that Ace ever read Benjamin Franklin's *The Way to Wealth*, but Franklin and Ace were kindred spirits when it comes to focusing on the little things. In 1758, Franklin wrote that Poor Richard "adviseth to circumspection and care, even in the smallest matters, because sometimes *a little*

neglect may breed great mischief; adding, *for want of a nail the shoe was lost; for want of a shoe the horse was lost, and for want of a horse the rider was lost,* being overtaken and slain by the enemy, all for want of care about a horse-shoe nail."

Ace and Franklin's message for leaders about the importance of focusing on the details is so powerful that I have a horseshoe hanging by a nail on a wall in my office.

Kevin McCallister (Macaulay Culkin) was only eight years old, but like Ace and Franklin, he knew that planning and details matter. Indeed, Kevin's attention to detail saved him from serious bodily harm and helped create one of the most popular movies of all time.

Written and produced by John Hughes (*The Breakfast Club, Ferris Bueller's Day Off,* and *Planes, Trains and Automobiles*), **Home Alone** was the second highest-grossing film of the year and would be the highest-grossing live-action comedy for the next twenty years. John Williams was nominated for two Academy Awards (Original Score and Original Song), two of his more than fifty music category Oscar nominations. The film was selected for preservation in the National Film Registry.

Kevin is accidentally left behind by his family in their Chicago home when they leave on a Paris holiday. Two burglars (the Wet Bandits, played by Joe Pesci and Daniel Stern) case out the McCallisters' neighborhood and decide to rob the McCallisters' house.

When Kevin learns that his house is a target of the two bandits, he first tricks them into thinking the family is still home (one of the best *faux* party scenes in the movies).

When they realize they've been tricked, the bandits discuss plans to break into the McCallisters' house on Christmas Eve. Kevin overhears them and prepares to defend himself.

Kevin's attention to detail is impressive. He defends his home castle using numerous home objects that he turns into creative weapons. The two bruised bandits finally corner Kevin in a neighbor's kitchen, but both are knocked-out cold by a spooky, but kind, neighbor (played beautifully by Roberts Blossom). All ends well for Kevin, but much less so for the two bandits.

In *Home Alone*, Kevin demonstrates impressive strategic planning and, with his personal safety and the sanctity of his home on the line, he perfectly executed his carefully thought-out and detailed plan that kept the bandits at bay.

If you think a successful strategy needs to be more complex than berries and blowtorches, then ***The Usual Suspects*** is your kind of film. Directed by Bryan Singer (*X-Men*, *Superman Returns*, and *Bohemian Rhapsody*) and written by Christopher McQuarrie (who wrote and directed several of the *Mission Impossible* movies), the film won two Oscars, for Actor in a Supporting Role (Kevin Spacey) and Writing (Original Screenplay). The plot is one of Hollywood's most intricate, and the film has become a classic crime thriller.

Keyser Söze ("the devil himself ") is a feared criminal legend whose identity is a mystery. Just the mention of his name intimidates even the toughest criminals. When a drug deal leaves one man alive who can identify him, Söze develops an intricate plan to kill him.

Söze's plan is so detailed that you may have to watch the movie a few times to figure it out. (After watching it a dozen or so times, I almost understand it.) The movie involves five New York criminals who, through a series of criminal events, unknowingly execute Söze's elaborate plan. After a number of violent escapades, the five end up conducting a crime they think they cooked up. But they aren't in control; Söze is the mastermind behind all of their activities.

The scenes that follow portray crimes within a crime, all of which keep the viewer off-balance and guessing about what really is happening. Finally, U.S. Customs agent Dave Kujan (Chazz Palminteri) conducts one of the greatest police interrogations in the movies. Kujan ends up releasing his suspect just as a description of Söze arrives in the police station. The movie ends with Kujan—and the audience—wondering, who really got away? (As one movie reviewer has written, "the ending has gone down as one of the greatest twists in movie history.")

Sometimes a leader's strategy can be so complex that even his colleagues don't quite understand it. When this happens, the odds of organizational success are significantly reduced.

CHAPTER FOUR

VISUALIZE IT: COMMUNICATE

Cool Hand Luke takes place in a rural Florida town where Luke Jackson (Paul Newman) is serving time in a state prison. (His fellow inmates nickname him Cool Hand after a card game.) The movie was nominated for four Oscars. Newman was nominated for Best Actor, and George Kennedy won the Oscar for Actor in a Supporting Role.

When Luke is working on a chain gang, he has a confrontation with a prison guard (a superb Strother Martin) who explains to Luke and the other convicts, "What we've got here is failure to communicate" (No. 11 on AFI's 100 Greatest Movie Quotes).

Failure to communicate clearly is the kiss of death for a leader's success.

Whether speaking or writing, clear communication is the *sine qua non* of effective leadership. A leader's success will often be determined by their ability to communicate effectively. Clear communication is also essential in establishing rapport with colleagues and coworkers, and developing and strengthening relationships.

Patrick Wilson, the Ford Professor of Artificial Intelligence and Computer Science at MIT, gave a popular lecture about the importance of communication. Wilson believed that no one should go through life without being armed with the ability to properly communicate. He told his students, "Your success in life will be determined largely by your ability to speak, your ability to write, and the quality of your ideas, in that order."

Napolean knew that clarity in communication was critical to success. The story goes that Napoleon had a corporal polish his boots when he discussed battle plans with his commanders. After they all agreed on the battle plan, Napoleon then would ask the corporal if he understood the plan. If the corporal didn't, Napoleon knew his chances of success in battle would be slim, as his troops probably wouldn't understand the plan, either. He would scrap the original plan and develop a new one.

My daughter Zoe is my corporal. When I began my public service in San Diego, the city's retirement plan staff was communicating with members with messages chock full of actuarial, legal, and pension jargon. So, the "Zoe rule" was born. It was simple: No communication could leave the office unless Zoe, then 14, could understand it.

As important as it is, communicating clearly is one of the leader's most difficult tasks. Osmo Wiio, a Finnish scholar who studied communication closely, observed that:

- If communication can fail, it will.
- If a message can be understood in different ways, it will be understood in just that way which does the most harm.

- There is always somebody who knows better than you what you meant by your message.
- The more communication there is, the more difficult it is for communication to succeed.

Several common behaviors lead to these organizational communication failures. One is a lack of interpersonal interactions, which is particularly acute in our age of remote work. Walking through an airport, I saw a coffee mug in a gift shop that had the following aphorism on it: "This Meeting Could Have Been an E-Mail." I got it. I've wasted a lot of time sitting through poorly run and counterproductive meetings. But, as Cal Newport wrote in *The New Yorker* almost a decade ago, "The dream of replacing the quick phone call with an even quicker e-mail message didn't come to fruition; instead, what once could have been resolved in a few minutes on the phone now takes a dozen back-and-forth messages to sort out. With larger groups of people, this increased complexity becomes even more notable."

Emails are the source of many miscommunications. It always amazes me how many interpretations a single sentence in an email can have. The fact is, nothing is more effective than face-to-face conversations and meetings. I constantly tell colleagues not to manage by email. To put it in terms of rock, paper, scissors, I think in-person conversations cover phone calls, phone calls blunt emails, and well-managed meetings cut them all.

Organizations succeed when colleagues communicate well and work collaboratively to achieve a common goal. For years, I have used the metaphor of a boat to encourage colleagues to get their co-workers together in person ("in the boat") to discuss issues as a team. In-the-boat meetings improve communication, reduce confusion, and lead to better outcomes. I design the office space to maximize the opportunity for boat meetings by adding conference rooms, huddle rooms, and open spaces where colleagues can get together to converse and collaborate. And, today, virtual boat meetings are just a click away no matter where in the world the participants might be.

The movie I use to illustrate getting colleagues in the boat is literally about that: ***The Boys in the Boat***.

Directed by George Clooney, the movie is based on the book *The Boys in the Boat: Nine Americans and Their Epic Quest for Gold at the 1936 Berlin Olympics* by Daniel James Brown. Brown's book tells the true story of an unheralded University of Washington rowing team that set its sights on participating in the 1936 Olympics.

It wasn't easy. After the Washington boat won the intercollegiate crew championship and qualified for the Olympics, the American Olympic Committee told them they would have to pay their own way to Berlin. With only one week during the Great Depression to raise $5,000, the Seattle community came together and raised the money in two days.

It was money well spent. When the boys and their boat got to Berlin, they won the gold medal. Eight individuals came together in a small space and worked together as a team. No matter how good each rower was individually, they had to row as one to win. (The actors who played the boys had no rowing experience and trained for months to prepare for the film.)

In-the-boat meetings increase the odds of operational success. They ensure that colleagues identify the skipper, get the right crew in the boat, work with their shipmates face-to-face, and chart a course that has a clear destination. Brown described the importance of assembling the right crew in his book: "Good crews are good blends of personalities: someone to lead the charge, someone to hold something in reserve; someone to pick a fight, someone to make peace; someone to think things through, someone to charge ahead without thinking It is an exquisite thing when it all comes together in just the right way."

And it's always better to have your colleagues in the boat with you when a decision is made rather than going it alone. Getting others' opinions, input, and buy-in is always preferable to going solo, particularly when colleagues and consultants are available to help discuss issues and complete projects. (For a harrowing example of going solo in a boat, watch Robert Redford in **All Is Lost**, an excellent movie and one of Redford's greatest performances, which suffered from a limited release and scant studio promotion.)

Of course, getting everyone in the boat doesn't guarantee a successful voyage. Group dynamics can lead to very bad decisions. Two common examples of group communication failures are groupthink and the Abilene Paradox.

Groupthink, now a popular part of the management lexicon, occurs when a group of intelligent people working together to solve a problem arrive at the worst possible answer. It most often occurs when the leader makes their position clear before the group discussion begins or when colleagues make a decision based on their desire to conform or avoid disagreement.

To avoid groupthink, leaders need to take special care not to subvert the group's decision-making and work hard to make sure that all meeting participants feel comfortable expressing their opinions without fear of retaliation or recrimination.

The Abilene Paradox occurs when a group agrees with a decision that none of them would make individually. Each thinks that their choice would be counter to the group's choice, so they go along even though they don't agree with the group's decision. Because of the Abilene Paradox, organizations too often take actions contrary to what the team really wants to do and defeat the very purposes the team is trying to achieve. (And why the *Abilene* Paradox? Because Jerry Harvey, a professor of management science at The George Washington University who first described the Paradox, was playing dominoes with his family in Coleman, Texas, when his father-in-law suggested that they all drive to Abilene for dinner.)

Charlie Granger, a character in the novella "Eve in Hollywood," one of six stories in *Table for Two* by bestselling author Amor Towles (*Rules of Civility*, *A Gentlemen in Moscow*, and *The Lincoln Highway*), reflects that "it is a funny aspect of life ... how a group of grown people can convince themselves to do something that none of them really want to do."

Charlie may not have understood it, but he was perfectly describing the Abilene Paradox.

Poor writing guarantees organizational miscommunications. Clear writing is a must to prevent misinterpretation. Simple, straightforward language ensures that the leader's message is more easily understood by their audience. But if you've ever sent a text or email that was misinterpreted, then you know how difficult it can be to clearly communicate in writing.

There are no shortcuts to effective writing. Almost four centuries ago, French philosopher Blaise Pascal wrote a friend: "The present letter is a very long one, simply because I had no leisure to make it shorter." (Hey, about a dozen drafts ago, this book was twice as long as what you're reading now.)

The economist and prolific author John Kenneth Galbraith knew that "the first draft is a very primitive thing. The reason is simple: Writing is difficult work. ... So all first drafts are deeply flawed by the need to combine composition with thought. Each later draft is less demanding in this regard. Hence the writing can be better." He added, "I've said many times that I do not put that note of spontaneity that my critics like into anything but my fifth draft."

Miss Beryl, Sully Sullivan's English teacher in Richard Russo's *Everybody's Fool* (Paul Newman plays Sully in the movie), teaches it: "Revise, revise, revise." She knows that "writing is thinking, and good, honest thinking involves revision."

Miss Beryl is right on both counts. Clear writing requires clear thinking. Galbraith noted, "It is impossible to be wholly clear on something you do not understand." Many written communications fail for the simple fact that the author doesn't quite know or understand completely what they are trying to say.

Complexity is another enemy of clear communication. Because I occasionally enjoy a martini (or two), I smiled when I read in *The New York Times* that a Brooklyn bar's "main cocktail menu will be compact, comprising just 10 or so drinks. Each will embody [the bartender's] belief that 'there's nothing as complex as simplicity.'"

Complexity often results when the communicator uses technical jargon that their audience doesn't understand, which is compounded by the fact that many of us are reluctant to ask questions for fear of looking dumb. During World War II, Winston Churchill relied heavily on Oxford physicist Frederick Lindemann for scientific advice. Why? Because Lindemann could translate complex scientific concepts into simple and understandable English. Lindemann could "decipher the signals from the experts on the far horizons and explain to me in lucid, homely terms what the issues were."

To improve my colleagues' written communications, I give each of them a copy of Strunk and White's *The Elements of Style*. (Rule 17: "Omit needless words.") The slim volume's sound advice echoes the 1917 *Kansas City Star* style sheet that taught Ernest Hemingway to "use short sentences. Use short first paragraphs. Use vigorous English.... Avoid the use of adjectives, especially extravagant ones."

Perhaps the most frequent cause of poor communication is that colleagues almost never see an issue or problem from the same perspective. I have a conference table in my office with a candy bowl in the middle of it. When colleagues sit at the table, each sees the bowl from a different angle and in a different light. It's the same with problems and projects. No one sees things in quite the same way.

Not a day goes by where two or more of my colleagues don't look at the same facts or issues but interpret them very differently. I've lost count of the number of times a colleague began a conversation with, "Well, from my perspective" or "I didn't see it that way." Of course. While we all may hear or read the same words, we often have very different takes on what those words mean.

This behavior is so endemic in the office that ***Rashomon*** is the movie I refer to the most. *Rashomon* was the first Japanese film to gain wide international acclaim, and many consider it one of the finest movies ever made. Directed by Akira Kurosawa (*Seven Samurai*), *Rashomon* won the Honorary Foreign Language Film Award at the Academy Awards for the most outstanding foreign language film release in the U.S. in 1951. The film is credited as the reason the Best Foreign Language Film Oscar category was created.

The movie is based on "In a Grove," a 1922 short story by Ryunosuke Akutagawa. Investigating the death of a samurai in a grove, the authorities interview the bandit Tajomaru, who admits to killing the samurai. But when they interview the samurai's wife, she, too, confesses to murdering her husband. Finally, reaching the murdered husband through a medium, he says he took his own life. So, the dead samurai, his wife, and the bandit all confess to being the killer. Kurosawa films *Rashomon* from four points of view: the bandit's, the samurai's wife, the samurai's, and a woodcutter (who witnessed the murder). Each of the four tells a different story.

So, who was the murderer? The movie ends with the woodcutter, sitting in a gatehouse during a rainstorm, saying that the bandit and the wife lied, but that the dead samurai, speaking through a medium, lied, too. A listener simply says: "It's human to lie. Most of the time we can't even be honest with ourselves."

Today, Wikipedia defines the "Rashomon effect" as when "an event is given contradictory interpretations or descriptions by the individuals involved, thereby providing different perspectives and points of view of the same incident."

Rashomon's message to leaders is simple: You must always remember that the odds of any colleague seeing something like you do are slim. Getting everyone to agree on the facts and the issues is a critical first step for organizational success. It takes time, patience, and very clear communication. But it is one of the most important parts of the leader's job.

CHAPTER FIVE

CAST IT: RECRUIT TALENT

It's a truism that an organization's human capital ultimately determines its success or failure. Evaluating, recruiting, and motivating talent is crucial for a leader to build a successful team.

Ron Ashkenas and Brook Manville observed that "people join organizations voluntarily, with the assumption that their participation is a two-way street. If they give their best efforts to achieve the collective goals that you lay out, they expect to be rewarded, in terms of compensation, growth, job satisfaction, relationships, and more. This is the basic social contract of organization life, and when it works, your team is more likely to perform at a high level with committed, loyal, and motivated people."

When rewards are not commensurate with organizational expectations and performance, a leader creates disengagement. Leaders reward colleagues and combat disengagement with more than money. They recognize and acknowledge achievements. They know the importance of creating opportunities for their colleagues' personal and career development. They engage colleagues by providing mentorship, regular feedback, and personal growth opportunities. And they give colleagues the autonomy to make decisions in their areas of expertise and trust them with meaningful responsibilities.

Influential leaders have the power to change the climate, the course, and the outcomes for their organization. Strong relationships transform vision into reality and potential into success.

In the final analysis, leadership is about relationships. Bridges built with authenticity, empathy, and good listening skills lead to trust. And trust leads to leadership.

As Larry Bossidy, the former senior GE executive and Chairman of Honeywell International, and Ram Charan, a distinguished corporate consultant, observed in their book, *Execution: The Discipline of Getting Things Done*, "Given the many things that businesses can't control, from the uncertain state of the economy to the unpredictable actions of competitors, you'd think companies would pay careful attention to the one thing they can control—the quality of their people, especially those in the leadership pool."

A movie where evaluating, recruiting, and motivating a talented team is critical to the plot's success is ***Ocean's Eleven***. Directed by Steven Soderbergh (*Sex, Lies, and Videotape*, *Erin Brockovich*, and *Traffic*) the cast includes George Clooney, Brad Pitt, Matt Damon, Andy Garcia, and Julia Roberts. Clooney reportedly sent the script to Roberts with a $20 bill and a note that said, "I hear you're getting 20 a picture now." At the time, Roberts was the highest paid female actor, making $20 *million* per movie.

Clooney plays convicted thief Danny Ocean; Julia Roberts plays his former wife; and Andy Garcia plays a casino mogul who owns three Las Vegas casinos. When Danny is paroled from prison, he comes up with a plan that involves all three of them, and the casinos.

To execute his plan, Danny sets out to recruit a talented team. His first recruit is his good friend Rusty (Brad Pitt).

Then, Danny recruits nine more professional thieves, each of whom smoothly demonstrates the specific skill necessary for Danny's plan to succeed: a blackjack dealer (Bernie Mac); a financier (Elliott Gould); two car experts (Scott Caan and Casey Affleck); an electronics expert (Eddie Jemison); a demolitions guy (Don Cheadle); a circus acrobat (Shaobo Qin); a wealthy hotel guest (Carl Reiner); and a pickpocket (Matt Damon). The movie highlights each thief's talent, and they execute their assignments to perfection. In the end, crime did indeed pay. But it took the right team to pull it off.

Like other successful leaders, Danny knew that recruiting the right team is a critical key to success. Leaders cannot succeed by themselves. Leading an organization is not a one-person show, no matter how much the media lionizes individual CEOs. When recruiting talent, leaders understand that they need to surround themselves with colleagues who are as good as or better than they are. Leaders who don't will struggle. Leaders need a team of colleagues who are motivated, loyal, and committed to the organization's vision and success. If they're honest with themselves, leaders know that most of their success is due to the talented colleagues around them.

The Adventures of Robin Hood stars Errol Flynn, Olivia de Havilland, Basil Rathbone, and Claude Raines. And although director Michael Curtiz (*Casablanca*) and star Flynn didn't like each other (one reason might have been that Flynn was married to Curtiz's ex-wife), the movie was nominated for four Academy Awards and won three. In 1995, it was selected for preservation by the National Film Registry.

Set in the late twelfth century, Robin Hood's adventures begin when the good King Richard the Lionhearted is captured and his brother, the treacherous Prince John, assumes the throne. When John oppresses the commoners, Sir Robin of Locksley—Robin Hood—takes up the fight. He robs the rich, gives to the poor, and woos Maid Marian. Robin Hood's refuge is Sherwood Forest, where he recruits his Merry Men to fight with him, including Little John and Friar Tuck.

Robin Hood and Little John first meet crossing a stream on a path only wide enough for one. When neither one will let the other pass, they come to blows, and Little John knocks Robin Hood into the stream. When Robin Hood wades to shore, Little John is afraid Robin will hold his loss against him. But, on the contrary, Robin tells him that he loves a man that can best him.

As Robin knew, surrounding oneself with colleagues who can best you is an important part of a leader's job.

One of my favorite movies that always reminds me about the importance—and joy—of surrounding yourself with talent is **The American President**. Directed by the great Rob Reiner (*When Harry Met Sally*, *Misery*, and *A Few Good Men*) and written by Aaron Sorkin, the movie stars Michael Douglas as widowed President Andrew Shepard.

Shepard becomes smitten with Sydney Ellen Wade (Annette Bening), a Washington lobbyist. For their first date, Shepard invites Sydney to a White House state dinner for the president of France and his wife.

During dinner in the East Room with the French couple, Shepard realizes that no one at the table speaks French, except Sydney. She begins speaking flawless French with the French president and his wife. Both immediately brighten, and the conversation begins to flow. Seeing Sydney's interaction with the French couple, Shepard bursts with pride knowing that Sydney is his date.

That's exactly how I feel when one of my colleagues distinguishes themselves. I smile and think with pride, that's my colleague!

Another important role of the leader is to make sure that everyone is cast in the role that best suits their talents. The title of the Spanish film *Palm Trees in the Snow* is a simple but powerful metaphor about putting the right people in the right place.

When I lived in Wisconsin, there was a beautiful pine tree in the backyard. It was majestic year-round, especially during wintertime when its boughs were covered with snow. Then I moved to San Diego and had three beautiful palm trees right outside my front door. They were a classic year-round California sight.

So, what did my pine tree and palm trees have to do with people management? Plenty.

If I transplanted the Wisconsin pine outside my San Diego front door, it would be dead in months. Likewise, if I transplanted my three San Diego palm trees to my Wisconsin backyard, they, too, would be dead in no time.

Like pine and palm trees, each of us needs to be planted in an environment where we can succeed. Leaders must honestly assess their colleagues' strengths and weaknesses and make sure that they are in positions that match their talents and where they can succeed. If they're not, even the most talented employee will struggle.

A bus is another management metaphor about a leader's role in managing talent. Two of the most successful leaders in sports both use the image of a bus to drive home (OK, pun intended) one of their most important responsibilities.

Nick Saban, the most successful coach in college football history, used a bus to explain one of his most important tasks: "If everybody does not buy into the same principles and values of the organization at the same high standard, you are never going to be successful. My goal ... is to get the right guys on the bus, get them in the right seats, and get the wrong guys off the bus."

At a conference where I spoke (I got the unenviable speaking slot following Mike "Coach K" Krzyzewski, Duke's Hall of Fame basketball coach), Coach K also used a bus metaphor to make a poignant and powerful point about surrounding yourself with the right people. Before his first day of high school, his mom called him into the living room. She said now that he was going to high school, he had to make sure that he got on the right bus. He told her that he knew his Chicago neighborhood well enough to get on the right bus to take to school. But his mom said that wasn't the bus she was talking about. She told her son that the bus she was talking about was the bus that he was going to drive for the rest of his life.

Only put good people on your bus, his mom said, and only get on a bus driven by a good person. The reason being? Because he would never accomplish what he wanted by doing it alone, and he would accomplish only what he wanted by surrounding himself with great people. Coach K said it was the best advice he ever got.

My favorite bus movie is ***The Fugitive***. (*Speed,* starring Keanu Reeves, Sandra Bullock, and Dennis Hopper, is a close second). Directed by Andrew Davis (*Under Siege, A Perfect Murder,* and *Holes*) and starring Harrison Ford and Tommy Lee Jones along with a superb supporting cast, *The Fugitive* was nominated for seven Academy Awards, including Best Picture. Jones won the Oscar for Actor in a Supporting Role.

Harrison Ford plays Dr. Richard Kimble, a Chicago surgeon who is wrongfully convicted of murdering his wife. While Kimble is on a bus that is taking him to prison, the bus is involved in an accident, and Kimble escapes. He then sets off to prove his innocence. Tommy Lee Jones, who plays Deputy U.S. Marshal Samuel Gerard, leads the chase to hunt Kimble down.

Successful leaders must be skillful bus drivers. They need to make sure that the right people are on the bus, that they are in the right seats, and that the wrong people get off the bus.

Bridging the gap between potential and performance requires a leader's strategic insight. Jack Welch, the legendary CEO and Larry Bossidy's mentor, focused on finding the right people (like Bossidy) and then giving them the tools to be successful. Welch said, "Before you are a leader, success is all about growing yourself. When you become a leader, success is all about growing others."

Identifying potential requires looking beyond current performance and learning to recognize the people who have the potential to grow and adapt for tomorrow, not just the ones who look good on paper today. The ability to do so can become one of the leader's greatest assets. Like George Bernard Shaw wrote, it means seeing what a colleague could be, even when it's not immediately evident. Assessing a colleague's untapped potential includes evaluating their initiative, adaptability, communication, resilience, and self-motivation. Personality and skills assessments can play an effective role in the evaluation process and help provide a more comprehensive view of performance and potential.

A leader also must distinguish between talent and ability. Talent is what people are naturally gifted with, while ability is the willingness to work to utilize that talent. People are born with innate skills, but leaders hone their skills through effort, discipline, and focus. While we have no control over what talent we're born with, we do have total control over the ability we put towards growing our talent.

The distinction between talent and ability also is crucial when identifying leadership potential. Some individuals may possess natural charisma or intelligence, but it's their work ethic and dedication to honing these natural skills that reveal true leadership capability. Leaders must assess their colleagues' inherent talent and how effectively they are working to develop it.

While it can be tempting to hire someone based on their current qualifications, leaders must think long-term. Identifying those who can grow into a role, contribute in new ways, and adapt to future challenges is often a better strategy than hiring based solely on a colleague's current skill set.

Finally, there's the importance of feedback. A leader isn't doing anyone a favor by not providing colleagues with constructive and candid feedback. Frequent dialogue with colleagues about their performance is critical for their and the organization's success. If someone doesn't know where they need to improve and grow, they won't. To be successful, an organization must have a process in place to provide regular feedback to staff, and every staff member needs feedback to successfully manage their career.

I have been in countless conversations with colleagues who candidly assess the performance of one of their employees with me, but then never share that feedback with the employee. When I was on my law firm's personnel committee, we met quarterly to review our associates' progress. At one meeting, the conversation made it clear that one associate was struggling and their long-term future with the firm was bleak. When I asked my partners who was going to share our assessment with the associate, they looked at me like I was nuts. No one was. Then they told me that if I felt strongly about it, then I could. Well, I did. I had lunch with Bill, and we had a candid conversation during which Bill acknowledged that he didn't find law practice very enjoyable and didn't think he was very good at it. No problem, I said: "You don't have to leave the firm anytime soon, and no one will know about this conversation."

We then put a job search plan in place, and it worked. Bill went into the legal department of a local Fortune 500 firm with the long-term intention of moving into the business side of things. Within a year, he moved into an operating unit and went on to a long and lucrative business career.

But no matter what performance evaluation process an organization uses (I eliminated written evaluations in mine), employees must understand that feedback is a two-way street. While the organization has a responsibility to provide meaningful and candid feedback to its employees, employees must understand that they, too, have responsibility for seeking feedback.

The movie I use to underscore this point is ***Miracle on 34th Street***. Why *Miracle on 34th Street*, you ask? Well, first, it's a classic holiday movie most people are familiar with. Kris Kringle is hired by Macy's to play Santa Claus—but he insists that he really is Santa Claus. It results in a great courtroom trial to determine if Kris really is Santa Claus. The movie was nominated for Best Motion Picture and won three Oscars. Edmund Gwenn, who played Kris Kringle, won the Oscar for Actor in a Supporting Role. Maureen O'Hara, the female lead, said that when children asked her if she was the lady that knows Santa Claus, she always answered, "Yes, I am. What would you like me to tell him?"

But the management principle the movie's title underscores for me is that, like 34th Street, feedback is a two-way street. It goes both ways. While the organization has a responsibility to provide meaningful feedback to employees, I tell employees that they shouldn't wait for their supervisor to provide feedback. They should proactively ask for it. There is no benefit to an organization's open-door policy if employees don't take the initiative to walk through the door.

But no matter how talented a leader may be or how positive the feedback they receive, careers seldom follow a straight path to the C-suite. There are many ups and downs and highs and lows. Office politics are dicey, mentors disappoint, and projects fail.

It's how a leader responds to career challenges that will determine their ultimate success.

Continuing to learn and grow is a critical component of career success. Successful actors don't become A-listers

or star in blockbusters all by themselves. They utilize many coaches to help them improve their talents and navigate their careers.

Leaders should too. It is a strength and not a weakness to seek advice and counsel. Successful leaders often retain an experienced career counsellor or coach. A professional who knows you and your organization can be an effective sounding board to discuss work-related challenges and keep you on track on your career path.

An executive coach can help leaders engage in self-reflection, an attribute that can help the leader become more resilient. Coaching also fosters authentic leadership that inspires teams to trust and follow leaders through difficult changes. Leaders who understand themselves better can better manage their reactions, communicate more effectively, and make thoughtful decisions. This clarity enables them to lead change with confidence, creating a more stable and supportive environment for their teams.

An executive coach can also improve a leader's emotional resilience. Leaders who develop their own capacity to stay calm and focused in the face of change can transfer that same mindset to their colleagues. This resilience creates a culture of perseverance and grit, which is essential for sustaining momentum during difficult periods of change. When leaders model mental toughness, their teams learn to trust the process and push through uncertainty.

CHAPTER SIX

CREW IT: ENGAGE EMPLOYEES

Leaders need engaged employees to achieve organizational success. Engaged employees get things done. They take responsibility. They make decisions. They are comfortable taking charge. Engaged employees improve organizations. The more engaged the group, the better the organization's performance.

According to a prominent project management firm, an engaged employee "is motivated to work hard towards a common goal that is in line with the company's vision. They will be committed to the values their organization represents. Engaged employees will have a clear view and understanding of the objectives of the work they are doing." Engaged employees also work harder because achieving a goal bigger than themselves expands them personally. No task seems beyond the reach of an inspired team member.

Engagement creates loyalty, and loyalty gives a leader the freedom to move beyond the burdens of transactional leadership where employees work only for monetary rewards.

Employees are more committed when they see personal benefits aligning with organizational goals. When leaders communicate how achieving the organization's mission can also help employees fulfill their personal aspirations, they foster deeper engagement and loyalty.

So, how do leaders foster engaged employees? Tom Peters noted, "The simple act of paying attention to people has a great deal to do with productivity." Leaders spend time with colleagues and get to know them, give them the means to do their jobs, provide a career path with training and development opportunities, encourage teamwork, make sure they understand the organization's mission and vision, communicate the organization's successes, empower them, and recognize their efforts.

The movie I keep in mind when I think about employee engagement is ***The Wizard of Oz***, one of the most popular movies of all time. It was added to the National Film Registry by the Library of Congress in 1989. It was nominated for six Academy Awards and won two, including the Oscar for Best Song, "Over the Rainbow."

Directed by Victor Fleming (*Gone with the Wind*) and based on the book by L. Frank Baum, the movie stars

Judy Garland as Dorothy Gale, who lives with Auntie Em and Uncle Henry in rural Kansas. When a tornado hits, Dorothy is knocked unconscious and has a dream that lands her in the magical land of Oz, where she sets off on a journey down the Yellow Brick Road to Emerald City to see the Wizard so she can get back to Kansas.

On the way, Dorothy and her dog Toto meet a brainless scarecrow (Ray Bolger), a heartless tin woodman (Jack Haley), and a cowardly lion (Bert Lahr). Each joins Dorothy hoping that the Wizard can help them, too. On her journey to Oz, Dorothy defeats (melts!) the Wicked Witch.

When Dorothy and her three friends finally arrive in Emerald City, they discover that the Wizard is a fraud. But he is a charming fraud: He gives a diploma to the Scarecrow, a medal of valor to the Lion, and a heart-shaped watch to the Tin Man, enhancing the self-esteem of each. But he can't do anything to get Dorothy home.

Just as Dorothy begins to think that she will never get back to Kansas, the Good Witch Glinda magically appears from the heavens in a big bubble with a magic wand in her hand. She tells Dorothy that she has always had the power to return home, she just had to learn it for herself. With Glinda's encouragement, Dorothy taps the heels of her ruby slippers (now on display at the Smithsonian Institution's National Museum of American History) together three times and repeats, "There's no place like home." Magically, she and Toto are transported back to Kansas.

Dorothy's scene with Glinda is one of my favorites. Why? Because of the magic wand in Glinda's hand. I want employees to believe that they, too, have a magic wand in their hand when they are at work. I mention the magic wand frequently to remind colleagues that they can make decisions and make things happen.

I recently promoted a colleague to an important job, and we meet each Monday to review the past week's activities and to plan for initiatives ahead. During one of these meetings, I asked her what she did over the weekend.

She said she had visited her mom, and that when her mom asked her about work, she replied, "Well, if I had a magic wand, I would … "

I immediately said, "Let me stop your right there." (According to my colleagues, this is one of my favorite phrases.) I told her, "You do have a magic wand. What do you want to do with it?" Well, she shared her ideas, and I asked her what she needed to achieve them. She told me, and she got them. Empowered with permission and resources, she achieved her goals, and the organization was much better for it.

One movie that is all about employee engagement is **_Norma Rae_**. Indeed, I'll go out on a limb here and say that there may not be a more engaged employee in film than Norma Rae Wilson.

Directed by Martin Ritt (_Hud_ and _The Great White Hope_), the film was nominated for four Oscars, including Best Picture. Sally Field won the Oscar for Actress in a Leading Role. (Field's Norma Rae was based on the real-life Crystal Lee Sutton, who participated in a 1974 union organizing campaign at the J. P. Stevens Mill in Roanoke Rapids, North Carolina.)

The movie begins when a New York labor organizer, Reuben Warshawsky (Ron Leibman), arrives in town to try to organize the mill's workers. Reuben meets Norma Rae, who becomes all in for the union. Her life will never be the same again.

As the movie deftly details, union organizing in the South is tough. Norma Rae's own father Vernon

(Pat Hingle) believes that New York labor leaders are Communist agitators that cost workers their jobs. (Later in the movie, Norma Rae's union activities indeed do get her fired.) And the movie similarly shows how difficult it was for Norma Rae to find a location to hold a union meeting where Blacks and whites could sit together.

But Norma Rae's work pays off: When the union election is held, the employees vote in favor of the union.

Before Rueben returns to New York, Norma Rae tells him, "I think you like me!" Field famously repeated this line at Academy Awards when she won the Oscar for *Places in the Heart*.

Norma Rae dramatically demonstrates the power of a passionate employee (even though that passion was driven by bad leadership). Her actions, both in words and symbolism, are powerful and have great impact on her co-workers.

Passionate employees are worth their weight in gold. A leader just needs to make sure that their own behavior promotes positive passion that is focused on the organization's success.

Another movie where a passionate employee has the courage of her convictions and the courage to express them is **Zero Dark Thirty**. A Best Picture nominee, the film was directed "brilliantly" by Kathryn Bigelow, the first woman to win an Oscar for Best Director (*The Hurt Locker*).

The film is a fictionalized account of the hunt for Osama bin Laden, and its focus is on Maya (played by Jessica Chastain, an Oscar nominee for Actress in a Leading Role), the CIA agent who doggedly hunted down Osama bin Laden's location in Pakistan, leading to the mission that killed him.

Maya is obsessed with finding bin Laden and, after years of tedious and painstaking investigative work, she identifies a compound in Pakistan where she is certain bin Laden lives. A meeting is finally scheduled with the Director of the CIA (James Gandolfini) to assess Maya's intel. Maya doesn't get a seat at the table; she's told to sit in a chair against the wall. She is the only woman in the room.

Days later, the president authorizes the mission to raid the compound. Navy SEALs helicopter in and find bin Laden on the third floor of the compound and kill him.

While the CIA leadership portrayed in the movie leaves something to be desired, Maya's character shows confidence and courage that are impressive. She thinks independently and speaks up to express the courage of her convictions.

Leaders and organizations need more Mayas. In my experience, the most important thing a leader can do to improve organizational communication is to ensure that colleagues can be honest and speak up without fear of retribution. But it is never easy for subordinates to be honest with their superiors and, too often, employees are afraid to speak up.

A leader must make it easy for co-workers to be honest. It is critical that a leader rid the workplace of fear, encourage staff to speak up, and reward them when they do. As Warren Bennis, one of the world's leading experts on leadership and Founding Chairman of The Leadership Institute at the University of Southern California, notes, "The basic problem in most organizations today, both public and private, is that they work to block transparency. Most are conveniently designed so that everyone seems to know what's wrong—but nobody admits it or tells anyone. . . . Exemplary leaders reward dissent. They encourage it."

Of course, there is a good reason many employees don't speak up. A *New Yorker* cartoon makes the point with humor. A young subordinate stands in front of a senior executive who is sitting behind an enormous desk. The caption has the senior executive telling the subordinate, "I'd like your honest, unbiased, and possibly career-ending opinion on something."

Shooting the messenger is nothing new. Sophocles wrote in *Antigone* that "no one loves the messenger who brings bad news," and Plutarch tells us that Tigranes beheaded the messenger who gave him bad news of a battle. ("The first messenger, that gave notice of Lucullus' coming was so far from pleasing Tigranes that, he had his head cut off for his pains; and no man dared to bring further information. Without any intelligence at all, Tigranes sat while war was already blazing around him, giving ear only to those who flattered him.") Not surprisingly, Tigranes lost the war. And in *Anthony and Cleopatra* Shakespeare writes that when Cleopatra was told that Mark Antony had married another, she threatened the messenger, who bravely replied, "I that do bring the news made not the match."

I've been "shot" several times for speaking up. One time occurred when my company invested $150 million (back in the day when $150 million was real money) in a critical IT project. At first, I had nothing to do with the project but word around the office was that it wasn't going well. Then I got an assignment that involved me in the project. After I had confirmed that the project was indeed seriously off track, I wrote a confidential memo sharing my findings with other senior managers. Shortly thereafter, the CEO called a meeting and, looking directly at me, said, "I will personally punch anyone in the nose who criticizes this project." After the meeting, another colleague told me that the company didn't need any "chicken littles."

Well, several months later, the company shut the project down, wrote off the entire $150 million, and the "punch me in my nose" CEO retired. (Ironically, he was succeeded by my colleague who chastised me for being a chicken little.) And nobody ever came to me afterwards and said, "Gee, David, you were right. Maybe we should have listened to you." Thankfully, I had already accepted a better job at a better company.

CHAPTER SEVEN

FINANCE IT: ENCOURAGE OWNERSHIP

Too many cooks do, indeed, spoil the broth. Too many organizational failures can be traced directly to too many manager-cooks in the kitchen with no one manager-chef in charge.

Just like movies, which have many actors and crew but just one director (producers, like board members, are another matter!), organizations have many employees, but each project require just one owner, the one person who is ultimately responsible for its outcome, to ensure success.

Early in my career, I reported to an exceptional CEO and leader who constantly stressed ownership. He asked, "If I need to know the status of a project and can only make one call, who am I going to call?" That colleague, he said, owns it. My CEO didn't know it, but his management mantra mirrored one in ***Ghostbusters***. Starring Bill

Murray, Dan Aykroyd, and Harold Ramis as oddball parapsychologists who start a ghost-catching business in New York City, *Ghostbusters* was the No. 1 box-office film for seven weeks and 1984's second highest-grossing film. It was the highest-grossing comedy ever until *Home Alone* was released in 1990. In 2015, it was selected by the Library of Congress for preservation in the National Film Registry.

Ray Parker Jr.'s iconic theme song sets the tone, and the Ghostbusters' prediction of a disaster of biblical proportions, with the possibility of dogs and cats living together, makes the movie a comedy classic. But what makes *Ghostbusters* a management classic is that when New York's mayor assesses the crisis, including millions of hysterical citizens, and has to decide who to call, he tells his aides to get him the Ghostbusters.

Nothing defines ownership—or the owner— better than the person who is on the other end of the line when the leader can only make one call. That person is the owner, the one person who has the ultimate responsibility to deliver the results the leader expects.

Apollo 13 is another movie that depicts the importance of an individual project owner. Directed by Ron Howard (Opie on the 1960's *The Andy Gritth Show*; he also directed *Parenthood*, *A Beautiful Mind*, and *Frost/Nixon*), *Apollo 13* recounts the story of one of the most dramatic space missions of all time. Based on *Lost Moon*, the 1994 memoir coauthored by Apollo 13 Commander Jim Lovell (played by Tom Hanks in the movie), *Apollo 13* was nominated for nine Academy Awards, including Best Picture, Actor in a Supporting Role (Ed Harris), and Actress in a Supporting Role (Kathleen Quinlan), and it won two.

On April 13, 1970, Apollo 13 blasts off from the Kennedy Space Center. It's the seventh Apollo mission and the third scheduled to land on the moon. Two days into the flight, an oxygen tank explodes and disables the spacecraft's electrical and life-support systems.

Instead of a lunar landing, the mission became solely about returning the crew to earth alive. While Hanks utters one of cinema's most famous lines ("Houston, we have a problem"— No. 50 on AFI's 100 Greatest Movie Quotes), the star on the ground is Gene Kranz, played by Ed Harris.

After disaster struck, it was chaos at Mission Control. But Kranz, NASA's chief flight director, takes charge (he owns the problem) of saving the Apollo 13 crew. Kranz takes ultimate ownership: He organizes the staff, prioritizes the projects, and leads the team that does the work. When President Nixon calls NASA for a mission status report, it's Kranz who provides it.

Kranz insists that the team focus on the problem and not make things worse by guessing. He asks them to do the impossible, and they do. Four days after blasting off, Apollo 13 and its crew splash down safely in the South Pacific.

Kranz and his team received the Presidential Medal of Freedom for their actions. (You can see the Apollo 13 command module *Odyssey* at the Cosmosphere space museum in Hutchinson, Kansas.)

Luckily, most leaders will never be responsible for a project as public and dramatic, with lives hanging in the balance, as Gene Kranz was. But all leaders will have to guide their organization on a myriad of mission-critical projects that can't fail, with all the pressure that entails.

As with Gene Kranz, the leader's ability to navigate those pressures and pitfalls will be the difference between the project's success or failure. Keeping calm, focused, and disciplined, and inspiring others to do likewise, is one of the true measures of a leader.

Ford v. Ferrari also drives (OK, another intended pun) home the importance of having one person in charge. Directed by James Mangold (*Star Wars: Dawn of the Jedi*, *Indiana Jones and the Dial of Destiny*, and *Girl, Interrupted*), the movie received four Oscar nominations, including Best Picture, and won two.

The film's focus is Henry Ford's obsession with beating Enrico Ferrari and the Ferrari racing team at Le Mans. Matt Damon stars as Carroll Shelby and Christian Bale as Ken Miles, who drives the Ford car. (At about the time of the actual Le Mans race, Ford unveiled the Mustang, and the real-life Miles told Henry Ford that the new car looked like a secretary's.)

After his team disappoints in an early race, Ford threatens to fire Shelby and his team. But Shelby isn't intimidated. He tells Ford that bureaucracy is killing the project and that you can't win a race by committee. One man needs to be in charge.

After reflecting on Shelby's comments, Ford gives him total control of the team, and the movie ends with the Ford team sweeping Ferrari's as Le Mans.

So, too, in business. While committees and consensus are important (remember "get in the boat"), ultimately one individual must be in charge and responsible for a project's success.

Of course, taking ownership also means taking responsibility. In *Moneyball*, Billy Beane is a leader who is unafraid to take responsibility for a tough decision. When he trades a player, he tells the player himself, face to face.

This wasn't the case with the leadership of the Durham (North Carolina) Bulls in ***Bull Durham***. Written and directed by Ron Shelton (*Tin Cup*), who received an Oscar nomination for his original screenplay, *Bull Durham* is an all-time great baseball movie and one of Kevin Costner's finest performances. It also was the first of a string of other great movies about baseball: *Major League*, *Field of Dreams*, and *A League of Their Own*. Costner also starred as Ray Kinsella in *Field of Dreams*.

Costner plays Bulls catcher Crash Davis, who has spent twelve years in the Minor Leagues ending up playing for the lowly Single-A Bulls, tasked with mentoring the organization's best pitching prospect, Ebby "Nuke" LaLoosh (Tim Robbins).

But when Nuke gets called up to "the show," the Bulls don't need Crash. Skip (the Bulls' manager, played by Wilford Brimley) calls Crash into his office to tell him that "the organization" wants to make a change.

When I heard Skip tell Crash that "the organization" wanted to make a change, I cringed. Putting the blame for a difficult decision on the nameless and faceless ("they" or "the organization") is a real hot button for me. It avoids any individual accepting personal responsibility and is particularly effective for assigning blame to no one. I hate it. Someone made the decision, and I think they should take responsibility for it.

Early in my career, I was responsible for my company's underperforming call centers that were located across the country. After a thoughtful analysis, the business decision was clear: My team and I agreed that we needed to close several of the centers. That decision was easy. Then, I asked the team how we were going to communicate the decision to the affected call center employees. No one said a word. Finally, someone suggested that we send a memo to the call center managers informing them of "management's" decision to close their center and let them handle it. Everyone agreed, except for me. I didn't like blaming "management" for a decision that I had made. Management didn't make the decision; I did.

So, I traveled to each affected call center and personally told the staff that I had made the decision to close the center. Neither "management," nor the "home office," nor "they" was to blame; I was—the guy standing right in front of them. After a few tears were shed, I explained what we were going to do to help each employee transition to a new job after the center closed. Not one employee left before we closed the doors for good.

I dislike the use of generic terms ("management") for the specific ("I") and ambiguous pronouns ("they") to replace the individual ("David"). Generic and ambiguous words create confusion. Too many times, in too many meetings, listening to too many conversations, I have observed the generic or indefinite diffuse personal responsibility and disperse accountability.

Listening to these conversations always brings to my mind another baseball classic: Abbott and Costello's comedy skit, "Who's on First?" As funny as it is, it's also relevant for leaders: We all have been in too many meetings and heard the same kind of dialogue.

Abbott: They give ball players nowadays very peculiar names.

Costello: Funny names?

Abbott: Nicknames, nicknames. Now, on the St. Louis team we have Who's on first, What's on second, I Don't Know is on third …

Costello: Well, then who's playing first?

Abbott: Yes.

Costello: I mean the fellow's name on first base.

Abbott: Who.

Costello: The fellow playin' first base.

Abbott: Who.

Costello: The guy on first base.

Abbott: Who is on first.

Costello: Well, what are you askin' me for?

Abbott: I'm not asking you—I'm telling you. Who is on first.

Costello: I'm asking you—who's on first?

Abbott: That's the man's name.

Costello: That's whose name?

Abbott: Yes.

Leaders need to make employees feel like owners. Leaders encourage individual responsibility. Leaders are clear and specific. Leaders know their people and their names.

CHAPTER EIGHT

FILM IT AND EDIT IT: EXECUTE EFFECTIVELY

Having a clear vision is one thing; turning it into reality is quite another. A leader must do both. What looks good on paper and sounds great in meetings doesn't guarantee success.

David Booth said it best: "Ideas are cheap. Execution is what's tough."

Even when a director has an inspiring idea, a well-written script, a talented cast and crew, and financing, a million and one things need to get done to produce a blockbuster. It takes strong production and execution to make it so.

Execution cannot be overemphasized. Paraphrasing the classic Budweiser slogan, when you say execution, you've said it all.

Decades before General Motors declared bankruptcy, a senior GM executive predicted it: "We have not achieved the success that we must because of severe limitations on our organization's ability to execute in a timely manner."

One business book I reread and recommend (other than this one) is Larry Bossidy and Ram Charan's *Execution*. In the book, they brilliantly describe how to link people, strategy, and operations together to get things done on time. Execution, they believe, is "a systematic process of rigorously discussing hows and whats, questioning, tenaciously following through, and ensuring accountability. ... It is a systematic way of exposing reality and acting on it."

Excellent execution, which includes focusing on fundamentals, paying attention to detail, and accomplishing the tasks at hand day in and day out, is the best predictor of an organization's success.

Recently, I read a dozen colleagues' critiques of our organization's enterprise risk management. When I finished, I could summarize them all in one sentence: "Someone somewhere sometime could make some kind of mistake." And that underscores the importance of execution: If everyone can properly execute their assignments, most risk evaporates. So, I continually stress that my colleagues focus on executing the job at hand. If they do, success usually follows.

Three of my favorite movies underscore the importance of execution—employees doing their jobs and doing them well.

Hoosiers is based on the actual 1954 Indiana state high school basketball championship that pitted the Milan Indians against the Muncie Central Bearcats. Milan won 32–30.

The movie stars Gene Hackman as Hickory High School's basketball coach, Norman Dale. Hackman didn't like the film and was difficult to work with on the set. He fussed with director David Anspaugh, and when Dennis Hopper arrived on the set, Hackman told him that the two of them would probably never work again after the movie was released.

But Hackman was wrong. *Hoosiers* went on to become one of the most popular sports movies of all time. And Dennis Hopper was nominated for an Oscar for Actor in a Supporting Role for his portrayal of Shooter, the troubled father of one of Hickory's players.

Coach Dale begins his practices with drills that focus on executing fundamentals. He doesn't have the players shoot, and they don't scrimmage. Dale's goal is to have five players on the floor functioning as one unit, one team, with no one player more important than another.

Executing the fundamentals and playing as a team, Hickory makes it all the way to the state championship game. With an enrollment of just over fifty students, Hickory plays the Bears of South Bend Central High School, one of the largest high schools in the state, for the state title.

With six seconds to go in the game, Hickory is down one with the ball. Coach Dale calls time-out and gathers his players around him to set up the last play. Then, . . .

Ok, did you think I was going to tell you who won? No way. You'll have to watch the film to see who wins and how!

Like Coach Dale, the Green Bay Packers' real-life head coach and NFL icon, Vince Lombardi, also believed in fundamentals and execution. Lombardi's favorite play was the Packers' power sweep, the epitome of execution. "There is nothing spectacular about it," Lombardi said. "It's just a yard gainer. [But] it's my number one play because it requires all eleven men to play as one to make it succeed, and that's what 'team' means."

One Packer commentator described the power sweep this way: "The pulling guards formed a convoy around end, with the lead guard taking out the cornerback and the offside guard picking up the middle linebacker or outside linebacker. The center executed [!] a cutoff block on the defensive tackle, and the onside offensive tackle popped the defensive end and then sealed off the middle linebacker. The blocking back led the ballcarrier into the hole with a down block on the defensive end, and the tight end drove the outside linebacker in the direction he wanted to go."

The Packers' power sweep is just a football play, but this is one of the best descriptions of execution I've ever read. One player said, "[The power sweep] made everybody work as a team. It gave everybody enough responsibility that you took it upon yourself to do the best you could." An opposing coach said, "It was merely execution. That sweep worked because everybody on the team did his job."

From the hardwood to the gridiron to the corner office, winners focus on executing the little things.

Vince Lombardi would have loved Erin Brockovich, someone who focuses on the details and executes her tasks to perfection. (It just so happens that Erin and I both hail from Lawrence, Kansas.) Directed by Steven Soderbergh, **Erin Brockovich** recounts the true story of Erin's (Julia Roberts) role in the legal battle against the Pacific Gas and Electric Company (PG&E) for contaminating groundwater near Hinkley, California. The film received five Oscar nominations, including Best Picture, Directing, and Actor in a Supporting Role (Albert Finney). Roberts won the Oscar for Actress in a Leding Role.

When Erin, an unemployed single mother with three children, is injured in a car crash, she sues and is represented by Ed Masry (Albert Finney). Erin loses her case, and Ed stops talking to her. Then one day, Ed comes to the office and finds Erin there. She needs a job, and he hires her.

Erin is assigned to work on a case involving PG&E and uncovers evidence that the company contaminated the groundwater in Hinkley. She tenaciously researches the facts and the law and visits numerous Hinkley residents, winning their trust.

Erin finds out that PG&E destroyed incriminating documents but uncovers others that they didn't. Erin's relentless research and close client relationships result in PG&E paying Hinkley residents more than $300 million in damages. Ed pays Erin a $2 million bonus.

Erin's work demonstrates the effort and dedication that execution requires and the results that excellent execution can deliver.

Another movie where execution leads to success is **Airplane!** When food poisoning lays low the pilots (Peter Graves and Kareem Abdul-Jabbar) and many of the passengers on a flight to Chicago, the plane must be landed by passenger Ted Striker (Robert Hays), a traumatized military veteran pilot who is haunted by bad war memories.

With great performances by Barbara Billingsley, Lloyd Bridges, Julie Hagerty, Leslie Nielsen, and Robert Stack (and a memorable scene starring Otto, the automatic copilot), *Airplane!* became one of the highest-grossing comedies in history. In 2010, *Airplane!* was selected for preservation in the United States National Film Registry.

When I was the CEO of a large national broker-dealer, *Airplane!* was the movie I talked about the most with the firm's registered representatives. In the heavily regulated securities industry, it was an entertaining and memorable example to drive home to investment professionals the importance of detailed execution and following procedures to a "T."

One reason that the *Airplane!* reference was effective was that it was simple to understand. I distilled the pilot's responsibilities to safely land a plane down to three tasks: flaps, wheels, and brakes. The pilot must adjust the flaps, lower the wheels, and put on the brakes. It's as easy, I said, as one-two-three. But, if the pilot does any of the three in the wrong order, then the plane will crash. So, do it the right way (flaps, wheels, brakes) and you'll execute the perfect landing every time.

For a real-world example of great execution of flaps/wheels/brakes, watch ***Sully***, the Clint Eastwood-directed film starring Tom Hanks. Hanks plays Chesley "Sully" Sullenberger, the U.S. Airways pilot who successfully lands Flight 1549 on the Hudson River after the plane's engines are disabled by a flock of birds after taking off from New York's La Guardia airport. One of the first things Sully and his copilot do after the engines begin to fail is to reach for the Airbus A320's flight manual and follow its emergency procedures. Doing so results in Sully's historic Hudson landing, which saves the lives of all 155 passengers and crew on board.

The flaps/wheels/brakes example also underscores the importance of prioritization. During a *Saturday Night Live* appearance, Steve Martin, one of the greatest entertainment talents of all time, told a joke that I often repeat to colleagues to emphasize the importance of prioritizing projects. "You can be a millionaire and never pay taxes! You say, 'Steve, how can I be a millionaire and never pay taxes?' First, get a million dollars." I've lost count of the number of times I've had to remind colleagues who get ahead of themselves and put the cart well ahead of the horse, to first get the million bucks.

One research study found that the common practice among the best corporate performers was that they mastered selectivity: "Whenever they could, they carefully selected which priorities, tasks, meetings, customers, ideas or steps to undertake and which to let go. They then applied intense, targeted effort on those few priorities. Talent, effort and luck undoubtedly mattered as well, but not nearly as much."

Dilbert comic-strip creator Scott Adams observed the same thing: "I can't see a correlation between the number of hours people work and promotion. What I do see is a correlation between success and the ability to communicate, the ability to focus on priorities."

But execution requires more than just a leader with a great idea. Execution also requires that leaders provide their colleagues with the proper financial, technological, and human resources, including access to knowledge, training, and support. Only by providing colleagues with the right resources will they be able to perform at their best.

Leaders have high expectations and set ambitious goals; that's their job. But ambitious goals can create overwhelming stress for colleagues. If leaders expect execution without considering the team's capacity, burnout can occur no matter how engaged the team is. To enhance execution and prevent burnout, workloads must be manageable, timelines must be realistic, and staffing must be adequate.

To manage stress, stepping back is often the key to moving forward. Encouraging employees to take guilt-free time off fosters a balanced, productive, and positive work environment. Leaders should model it by taking time off themselves. Clearing one's head allows space for reflection, recalibrating the best way forward, and uncovering innovative ways to help colleagues achieve successful execution.

CHAPTER NINE

MARKET IT:
MARKET ORGANIZATIONAL CHANGE

Benjamin Franklin (who else?) said it best: "When you're finished changing, you're finished."

While times of stability can be handled by managers, times of change require leaders. Harvard Business School professor John Kotter has written that managers promote stability while leaders press for change. "Management is about coping with complexity. ... Good management brings a degree of order and consistency to key dimensions like the quality and profitability of products."

But leadership, Kotter stresses, "is about coping with change Major changes are more and more necessary to survive and compete effectively in this new environment. More change always demands more leadership."

But as Machiavelli wrote in *The Prince* centuries ago, "It ought to be remembered that there is nothing more difficult to take in hand, more perilous to conduct, or more uncertain in its success, than to take the lead in the introduction of a new order of things."

In fact, even when they are faced with the knowledge that what they think is wrong or what they are doing can be done better, people still resist change. Bill James, the statistician who challenged and changed the baseball industry (and a Lawrence, Kansas resident), said, "When I was young and naïve, I assumed that when you demonstrated that something was false, everybody would say, 'Oh, I didn't know that' and stop doing what it was that had been demonstrated as being useless or counterproductive. Of course, the world doesn't work like that."

English economist John Maynard Keynes acerbically noted, "When the facts change, I change my mind. What do you do, sir?" But, as we see frequently even today, most people don't. John Kenneth Galbraith, another famous economist with three names, observed that, "faced with the choice between changing one's mind and proving that there is no need to do so, almost everybody opts for the latter."

But organizations must change to succeed and survive. Given today's rapid technological advances, an organization's business model and strategy can change overnight. A leader must recognize these advances and be prepared to implement changes to move the organization forward.

In the Best Picture winner **Annie Hall**, Alvy Singer (Woody Allen) explains to his girlfriend Annie Hall (Diane Keaton, who won the Oscar for Actress in a Leading Role) that relationships must constantly keep moving forward to flourish. Like relationships, organizations, too, must keep moving forward to remain relevant. If they don't, a breakup is inevitable.

When I explain to colleagues that change is certain, I quote Sonny, the hotel manager in **The Best Exotic Marigold Hotel**. The movie tells the story of seven retired English travelers who accept invitations to stay at the newly opened Best Exotic Marigold Hotel in Jaipur, India.

When the guests complain about the hotel's rundown condition and crappy food, Sonny tells them not to worry because everything will be all right in the end—and if it's not all right, then it's not the end.

My point to colleagues is that because organizations are never "all right," it can never be the end. Change is inevitable and always necessary for survival.

Marketing and selling organizational change effectively is the leader's biggest challenge.

But a leader just can't just try to manage change. Like a studio launching a marketing campaign when it releases a new movie, a leader must market change when they "release" it into the organization. While a leader is usually comfortable with change, colleagues and co-workers often aren't. The leader's biggest challenge is to convince them that change will be good for the organization and them. To do so, the leader must market it.

I am always surprised (and disappointed) that so few employees ever think change might affect them positively— although in so many cases it does. This fact always comes to mind when I am jogging and am passed by a cyclist because it reminds me of ***Breaking Away***.

Breaking Away's characters all experience change, and all for the better. One of the movie's most inspirational messages is that change is good!

Filmed in Bloomington, Indiana, with a low budget and unheralded cast, *Breaking Away* was a real sleeper. Steve Tesich won the Oscar for his original screenplay, and the movie was nominated for four more, including Best Picture.

The movie focuses on four Bloomington kids ("Cutters" in the local parlance because of the local limestone industry) who struggle with the gulf between themselves and Indiana University's wealthier fraternity boys. But the four Cutters and Dave's parents undergo profound and positive change.

Breaking Away underscores one of my messages to employees about change: It can benefit you if you embrace it. If employees can overcome their anxiety about change and accept its opportunities, they usually end up in a better place.

The challenge for leaders, of course, is that most people hate change. "Most of us are great with change, as long as it was our idea," says Chief Inspector Armand Gamache in Louise Penny's novel *Still Life*. The problem is that change is almost always someone else's idea.

Why is change so difficult for people? Human nature seems to focus on any possible negative consequence the change might have on the individual. Dr. Tamar Chansky notes that "how we thrive is through routine and predictability. It gives us a sense of control. When there are big changes, we are suddenly thrown into a state of uncertainty." A business coach observed that "little, even subtle [changes], can rattle today's workplaces."

Barbie is a movie all about change—and how much Barbie hates it. Directed by Greta Gerwig (the first female director to have three films, *Barbie*, *Lady Bird*, and *Little Women*, nominated for Best Picture) and written by Gerwig and Noah Baumbach, *Barbie* grossed more than a billion dollars in just two weeks, passing *Home Alone* as the highest-grossing comedy.

Barbie was the first toy-based movie to be nominated for Best Picture, and Ryan Gosling was the first actor to be nominated for portraying a toy. Shockingly, neither Gerwig nor Margot Robbie, who played Barbie, received an Oscar nomination.

But beyond *Barbie's* glitz and glamour, change and its challenges are themes that run throughout the movie. Barbie is terrified of change and never wants anything to change. But life is all about change. As another doll tells her, change is like being a human all the time.

Through her movie experiences, Barbie finally sees the positive possibilities in change and chooses to embrace change. As should colleagues and co-workers.

Another movie that involves resistance to change is ***The Hundred-Foot Journey***. The movie wasn't a blockbuster and didn't get glowing reviews. But one scene perfectly captures the need for change.

Helen Mirren plays Madame Mallory, the arrogant and haughty owner of a Michelin-starred restaurant in a French village. All is going well with Madame and her restaurant until an Indian family moves in across the street (one hundred feet away) and has the temerity to open an Indian restaurant.

Madame Mallory ultimately takes on one of the family as an apprentice who, unbeknownst to her, adds some additional spices to an ages-old Mallory recipe. When

Madame asks why would anyone change a recipe that is two hundred years old, the answer is a simple one: Maybe two hundred years is long enough.

For an organization to succeed, it must continuously improve. To do so, employees must be able to challenge the status quo. They need to know that just because something has always been done a certain way, that may not be the best way to do it in the future.

Leaders challenge the status quo by seeking different perspectives (think *Rashomon*) and constantly challenging colleagues by asking "Why?" and "What if?" Leaders, the journalist and author Warren Berger writes, want "the people working around them to be more curious, more

cognizant of what they don't know, and more inquisitive—about everything, including 'Why am I doing my job the way I do it?' and 'How might our company find new opportunities?'"

I ask *why* so often that my colleagues often accuse me of managing like a four-year-old. Indeed, Berger notes that question-asking peaks at age four or five and then begins to drop off. As a result, when employees enter the workforce, many have gotten out of the habit of asking questions about what's going on around them.

In fact, one of the great advances in photography, Polaroid's instant camera, was inspired by the three-year-old daughter of its inventor, Edward Land. After her dad took her picture, his daughter was impatiently waiting to see it. Her dad told her that that the picture had to be processed first, and she asked: "Why?" That question prompted Land to search for a process that would eliminate waiting to see a picture.

But asking *why* is critically important and almost always leads to more thoughtful decisions. Questioning colleagues' assumptions and asking them why they are doing something in a certain way stimulates robust dialogue and tests the rationales that support current (status quo) practices and processes.

When I ask a colleague "Why?" their answer almost always includes "because." It happens so often that I have a "because" rule. If the answer *begins* with because ("Because we've always done it this way"), it usually indicates that my colleague hasn't given the matter much thought; it's just the way it's always been done. If, on the other hand, the answer ends with because ("We've always done it this way because ...") then chances are they have given this issue a good deal of thought and decided on the best way to proceed. "It's the way it's always been done" is the sign of lazy thinking. There almost always is a better way.

If I ask why and a colleague answers with three good reasons, it's generally an indication that they have thought the issue through. If I get three good reasons why, I won't second-guess their decision, even if I would have made a different one.

Being open-minded is another critical leadership skill. To facilitate change, a leader needs to be open-minded to ideas. As Tom Peters recognized, "The greatest difficulty in the world is not for people to accept new ideas, but to make them forget old ideas." (When silent pictures were popular, but sound was on its way, movie mogul Harry Warner asked, "Who the hell wants to hear actors talk?")

Keeping an open mind and overcoming biases and ingrained thinking is challenging. Since people only know what they know, left to their own devices, new projects to improve or replace current processes or procedures often result in very little actual improvement.

Another impediment to colleagues accepting change is fear—and not fear about how the change will impact the organization, but how the change will affect them personally. Leaders should never forget the fear and anxiety that any change will create in their organization.

Fear can be debilitating. In *The Wizard of Oz*, when Dorothy, the Tin Man, and the Scarecrow first run across the Cowardly Lion, the Lion scares them. But when the Lion snaps at Toto, Dorothy slaps him, and he dissolves into tears. Seeing his tears, Dorothy tells him that he's nothing but a great big coward. The Lion agrees; he says he even scares himself. When the Lion admits that he hasn't slept in weeks, the Tin Man suggests that he try counting sheep. The Lion says he's tried to, but it doesn't do any good. He's afraid of sheep.

And, let's face it, change can be painful. Oftentimes leaders must make tough decisions that come with significant pain today to ensure their organization's long-term viability. How many times have companies stuck to their original strategies, only to have their competitors and customers move beyond them? Just spend a few minutes reviewing the historical company components of the Dow Jones Industrial Average to see change over time.

One of the saddest cases is Kodak. Kodak's leaders weren't surprised by the digital revolution; they had known it was on the way for a long time. But even though they recognized the future challenge to their entire business model, they couldn't bring themselves to make the difficult changes necessary to adapt to new technologies. (How would you like to lay off thousands of chemical engineers in a company town the size of Rochester, New York?) Given Kodak's leaders' failure to change their product strategy and focus, the result was a long, painful, and inevitable road to bankruptcy.

Given the complex issues that change raises, leaders need to market their ideas about change. They need to communicate the reason for change and sell the rationale for the changes they want to make.

Harvard Business School Professor Rosabeth Moss Kanter's research found that "the best tool for leaders of change is to understand the predictable, universal sources of resistance in each situation and then strategize around them." Professor Kanter cited these common sources of resistance:

- Loss of control.
- Excess uncertainty.
- Surprise, surprise!
- Everything seems different.
- Loss of face.
- Concerns about competence.
- More work.
- Ripple effects.
- Past resentments.
- Sometimes the threat is real.

Professor Kanter concludes, "Although leaders can't always make people feel comfortable with change, they can minimize discomfort. Diagnosing the sources of resistance is the first step toward good solutions. And feedback from resisters can even be helpful in improving the process of gaining acceptance for change."

But no matter how well a leader markets change, some in the organization will never, ever accept it. While organization charts make lines of authority and reporting relationships look clear and orderly, the reality is quite different. There are employees on that chart who can have an outsized impact on a leader's and organization's effectiveness, often for ill. I call these employees Barzinis, and leaders need to be on the lookout for them.

I discussed *The Godfather* in Chapter Two, but the movie is so rich with management lessons, I will include another one here.

The mob war that broke out was bad for the crime business. To end the violence and get business back to normal, mob families met to negotiate a resolution to the conflict.

After the meeting, the Godfather and his consigliere are chauffeured home. During the ride, the Godfather pieces together the critical role played by another mob boss, Don Barzini.

Later in the movie, Michael confronts his brother-in-law who finally admits Don Barzini's role in Sonny's murder.

Like the Godfather, a leader always needs to be mindful that they will have enemies in their organization. Not everyone will have the leader's best interests at heart. The key for a leader is to keep their eyes and ears open and identify them.

Who are these internal enemies? How can a leader recognize their organizational foes who are exerting negative influence or derailing important operations, projects, or strategies.

They are not slackers, and their influence is subtle and often difficult to identify. In my experience, they usually:

- Work in a core and critical function.
- Occupy a position just below senior management.
- Are long-tenured.
- Have relationships that influence others.
- Fear change.
- Lack a strong supervisor who can recognize and counter their influence.
- Avoid disagreeing with their seniors but creates doubts behind their backs with peers or subordinates.

Internal adversaries can subtly sabotage or torpedo a leader's decision or project. There's a powerful adversary on board in ***The Hunt for Red October***, a terrific movie based on the Tom Clancy novel. *The Hunt for Red October* stars Sir Sean Connery who plays Marko Ramius, the captain of the Soviet submarine *Red October*. The movie recounts the consequences of Ramius' intent to defect with the *Red October* to the U.S., which involves confrontations with submarine captains of the U.S. and Russian navies. Those captains are played to perfection by Scott Glenn and Stellan Skarsgård (Ramius' arrogant adversary, Russian captain Tupolev). Ramius learns that there is indeed a saboteur on board his boat. Unbeknownst to Ramius, a KBG spy is masquerading as a cook on the crew.

How do you neutralize an internal adversary? It's not easy. First, you must identify them (remember Steve Martin, "First, get a million dollars!"). Then, you can take the time to involve them early in projects and encourage their input, which can go a long way in building bridges and gaining their support. Engaging naysayers in planning can increase their commitment to supporting the project.

A strong culture with effective supervision, candid communication, and acknowledging and addressing legitimate issues can go a long way to counteract the adversary's influence. But a leader must be prepared to exit them from the organization. Too many CEO memoirs include descriptions of internal adversaries and the CEO's regret in not moving faster to fire them.

While there is no approach that can guarantee success in marketing organizational change, Atul Gawande writes that people follow the lead of others they know and trust when they decide whether to accept new ideas. "If they know you, they might trust you; and, if they trust you, they will change." So, sometimes, I just fall back on Eddie Murphy's advice to the Beverly Hills cops Sergeant John Taggart and Detective Billy Rosewood in **_Beverly Hills Cop_**: "Trust me!"

What are some effective ways to market change? None of the following suggestions will surprise you, but they shouldn't be overlooked.

- **Communicate clearly.** You can't communicate enough when change is necessary. When I introduce any organizational change, big or small, I take great care to try to communicate it effectively and paint a clear picture of the desired result. I hold one-on-one meetings with those most directly affected by the change. I hold small team meetings. I hold all-staff meetings. I send all-staff emails to explain the change and why we are introducing it. And after the announcements and implementation, leaders make sure that colleagues can share their feedback about the change.

- **Provide support.** Change often requires staff to do new things or do current tasks differently. Make sure that your colleagues are provided with the necessary training and resources to help them adapt to the change. This reduces anxiety and builds confidence.

- **Implement effectively.** How change is implemented often goes a long way to ensuring its success. Sometimes, you can implement the change over time and smooth the transition to the new state.
- **Celebrate successes.** It is critical to celebrate successes during any change. This helps colleagues see the benefit of the change.

Over time, if changes are well thought out, communicated effectively, and executed well, the skeptics will forget their initial aversion to the change. Many will often end up asking, "Why didn't we do this sooner?" And some may even seek to take credit for the idea!

Chapter Ten

It's a Wrap! Release a Blockbuster

If there's one thing Hollywood loves, it's a happy ending: Seabiscuit besting War Admiral at Pimlico, Patton liberating Bastogne, Apollo 13 successfully splashing down in the Pacific, the University of Washington boys in the boat winning the gold medal, or the underdog Hickory Huskers winning the Indiana high school basketball title.

I do, too.

And if I could share a bucket of popcorn with you and your leadership team and watch just one blockbuster with a happy ending that embodies all the leadership lessons discussed in this book, it would be *The Sting*.

Released on Christmas Day 1973, **_The Sting_** was directed by George Roy Hill and starred Paul Newman and Robert Redford. (They had worked together four years earlier in _Butch Cassidy and the Sundance Kid_, which was nominated for seven Oscars and won four.)

The Sting was nominated for ten Academy Awards and won seven, including Best Picture and Directing. Marvin Hamlisch won an Oscar for his scoring adaptation of Scott

Joplin's ragtime music. Redford received his only Best Actor Oscar nomination.

Set in Chicago in the thirties, *The Sting* involves an elaborate sting orchestrated by Henry Gondorff (Newman), a legendary con artist, and his protégée Johnny Hooker (Redford). Robert Shaw, who starred in *Jaws* the next year, plays Lonnegan, the mobster who is the object of the con.

Gondorff develops an elaborate plan to con Lonnegan, but the con is complex and requires assembling a team of experienced con men with individual skills to pull it off. And they succeed. The con is played to perfection by a brilliant cast and crew.

No Harvard Business School case study could describe it better. Gondorff is a leader who brilliantly produces a blockbuster. He

- **has a clear vision** (creates the con),
- **thinks strategically** (develops an effective plan to achieve his vision),
- **plans carefully** (no detail is too small),
- **visualizes the goal** (communicates clearly so that his colleagues see and share his vision),
- **casts and crews it to perfection** (assembles a talented team with each member bringing a unique skill and empowered to do their required tasks),
- **finances it** (each colleague takes ownership for a successful outcome),

- **films it** (executes the plan to perfection),
- **markets it** (each colleague understands and enthusiastically buys into the con), and, as a result, he
- **produces a blockbuster.**

But no matter how well a leader "scripts," "casts and crews," "finances," or "films" their organization, success isn't guaranteed. Leaders can't always produce a blockbuster. To improve the odds that they will, leaders should keep *Office Space* in mind.

Office Space was written and directed by Mike Judge (*Beavis and Butt-Head* and *King of the Hill*). It was his first feature film, and it was anything but a blockbuster. But after a modest start, *Office Space* has become a cult classic.

Like *Norma Rae*, *Office Space* depicts the results of terrible organizational leadership. The office is "a fluorescent-lit nightmare," and the movie is a "brutal portrayal of workplace misery." Peter Gibbons (Ron Livingston) plays a software engineer stuck in a cubicle jungle in a soulless office space. The only joy in his life is his love interest, played by Jennifer Anniston.

The root cause of the office's dismal working environment is, of course, lousy leadership. The boss, Bill Lumbergh (Gary Cole), does everything a boss shouldn't do. His abysmal leadership breeds disengaged and apathetic employees. If an organization exhibits these symptoms, the cause is usually a Bill Lumbergh in the building.

Another lesson that Bill Lumbergh humorously reinforces is that leaders shouldn't be jerks. And leaders shouldn't tolerate jerks. If they are, or do, ultimately, they will be torpedoed like captain Tupolev in *The Hunt for Red October*. Tupolev is so obsessed with besting his mentor that he recklessly fires a torpedo to destroy *Red October*. But the torpedo misses its mark and homes back in on Tupolev's own sub. Right before impact, and the impending obliteration of Tupolev's sub and crew, his second officer curses him, "You arrogant ass, you've killed us!"

We've all come across a Tupolev or two in our careers. Leaders shouldn't behave like Tupolev and shouldn't tolerate any colleagues who do.

I think one of the best tools a leader can use to improve the odds of releasing a blockbuster is the action plan. The influential CEO who taught me the importance of ownership was also a firm believer in action plans.

Every year, he would meet with the management team to agree on the organization's action plan for the following year. When the team was finished, the organization's key priorities had been identified, and every quarter the team met to review our progress toward achieving them. He also recommended that colleagues draft an action plan for any important project or goal. I've used action plans ever since.

Over the years, I have developed my own personal action plan that summarizes my goals:

- Ask why.
- Think and don't just do.
- Identify who's is in my boat.
- Communicate clearly.
- Identify who's on my bus, where they are sitting, and who needs to get off.

- Use my wand.
- Speak up and challenge the status quo.
- Determine which projects I own.
- Prioritize my projects—make sure I get a million dollars before I spend it.
- Execute.

If I follow this plan, my odds of producing a blockbuster are significantly improved.

Afterword

Thank you for reading our book. Tom Peters said, "If I read a book that cost me twenty dollars and I get one good idea, I've gotten one of the greatest bargains of all time." We hope that's just how you feel.

Tony and I hope the book's movie leadership lessons will help you be an even more effective leader and help you lead your organization to even greater success.

And now when you watch movies, we hope a scene or two will make you smile and think, "You know, I can use that at the office."

CLOSING CREDITS

Preface

Tom Peters, Goodreads.com.

Chapter One

George Bernard Shaw, *Back to Methuselah, In the Beginning*, Brentano's, 1921.

See fieldofdreamsmoviesite.com.

Nicole Perlroth, Sheera Frenkel, and Scott Shane, "Facebook Exit Hints at Dissent on Handling of Russian Trolls," *The New York Times*, March 19, 2018.

Nicole Perlroth and Sheera Frenkel, "The End for Facebook's Security Evangelist," *The New York Times*, March 20, 2018.

Chapter Two

Michael E. Porter, "What is Strategy?" *Harvard Business Review*, November–December 1996.

See International Churchill Society, WinstonChurchill.org. Steve Jobs, Goodreads.com.

Manohla Dargis, "Moneyball: Throwing a Digital Age Curveball," *The New York Times*, September 22, 2011.

Chapter Three

Colin Powell, Wikiquote: Quote of the Day, October 19, 2021.

Benjamin Franklin, "The Way to Wealth," *The Papers of Benjamin Franklin*, Vol. 7, October 1, 1756 through March 31, 1758, ed. Leonard W. Labaree, Yale University Press, 1963.

Colin McCormick, "The Usual Suspects Ending, Explained," screenrant.com, November 13, 2024.

Chapter Four

Justin Bariso, "A Respected MIT Professor Said Your Success Will Be Determined by 3 Things. Here's How to Get Better at Each of Them," *Inc. Newsletters*, May 2022.

Ben Carlson, "Napoleon's Corporal," awealthofcommonsense. com, April 6, 2016.

Wikipedia, "Wiio's Laws"; Jason Fried, "Osmo Wiio: Communication Usually Fails, Except by Accident," signalvnoise.com., April 22, 2008; and Wil Moushey, "A Primer on Wiio's Laws: Improving Communication," medium.com, September 9, 2019.

Cal Newport, "Was E-Mail a Mistake?" *The New Yorker*, August 6, 2019.

William H. Whyte, Jr., "Groupthink," *Fortune*, February 29, 1952; and Kathrin Lasslia, "A Brief History of Groupthink," *Yale Alumni Magazine*, January–February 2008.

Jerry B. Harvey, "The Abilene Paradox: The Management of Agreement," *Organizational Dynamics*, Summer 1988.

Amor Towles, *Table for Two*, Viking Press, 2024.

Blaise Pascal, *The Provincial Letters* (Letter XVI), December 4, 1656, translated by Thomas M'Crie, Robert Carter & Brothers, 1856.

John Kenneth Galbraith, "Writing, Typing, and Economics," *The Atlantic*, March 1978, and "John Kenneth Galbraith's Legacy and Lessons for Today," Panel Discussion, *UC Berkeley Journalism*, April 12, 2005.

Richard Russo, *Everybody's Fool*, Alfred A. Knopf, 2016.

Robert Simonson, "Mezcal Master Turns to the Martini,"

The New York Times, March 4, 2020.

Erik Larson, *The Splendid and the Vile: A Saga of Churchill, Family, and Defiance During the Blitz*, Penguin Random House, 2020.

William Strunk, Jr., and E. B. White, *The Elements of Style*, Fourth Edition, Pearson Education, 2000.

Albery Murray, *Stomping the Blues*, McGraw-Hill, 1976.

Chapter Five

Ron Ashkenas and Brook Manville, *The Harvard Business Review Leader's Handbook: Make an Impact, Inspire Your Organization, and Get to the Next Level,* Harvard Business Review Press (2018).

Larry Bossidy and Ram Charan, *Execution: The Discipline of Getting Things Done,* Crown Business, 2002.

Jack Welch, BrainyQuote.com.

Chapter Six

"How to Engage Employees—A Complete Guide for Managers," nutcache.com/blog/how-to-engage-employees/, April 10, 2017.

Tom Peters, Goodreads.com.

Manohla Dargis, "Zero Dark Thirty: By Any Means Necessary," *The New York Times,* December 17, 2012.

Warren Bennis, "A Corporate Fear of Too Much Truth,"

The New York Times, February 17, 2002.

Alex Gregory, *The New Yorker,* June 16 & 23, 2003. Sophocles, *Antigone,* Loeb Classical Library, 1912. Plutarch, *Life of Lucullus* (Dryden translation), para. 25, 1683. Shakespeare, *Antony and Cleopatra,* Act 2, Scene 5.

Chapter Eight

Chris Lazzarino, "The Long Game: David Booth's historic gift to KU," *Crimson & Blue*, Fall 2025.

Bill Vlasic, "After Bankruptcy, G.M. Struggles to Shed a Legendary Bureaucracy," *The New York Times*, November 13, 2009.

Larry Bossidy and Ram Charan, *Execution: the Discipline of Getting Things Done*, Crown Business, 2002.

Ed Gruver, "The Lombardi Sweep: The Signature Play of the Green Bay Dynasty, It Symbolized An Era," *The Coffin Corner*: Vol. 19, No. 5 (1997).

Morton T. Hansen, "How to Succeed in Business? Do Less," *The Wall Street Journal*, January 12, 2018.

Hal Lancaster, "Managing Your Career: Scott Adams Offers Valuable Lessons from Life with Dilbert," *The Wall Street Journal*, August 8, 1995.

Chapter Nine

Benjamin Franklin, BrainyQuote.com and Goodreads.com.

John P. Kotter, "What Do Leaders Really Do?" *Harvard Business Review*, March 1990.

Nicolo Machiavelli, *The Prince*, Chapter VI, translated by W. K. Marriott, FrHistS, J. M. Dent & Sons Ltd., E.P. Dutton (1908).

Tyler Kepner, "Baseball: Red Sox Have the Thinking Fan's Writer on Their Side," *The New York Times*, November 28, 2002.

John Maynard Keynes quote from remarks of Mark C. Williams, President and CEO, Federal Reserve Bank of New York, at the Ninth High-Level Conference on the International Monetary System, Zurich, Switzerland, May 14, 2019 (newyorkfed.org/newsevents/speeches/2019).

John Kenneth Galbraith, "Came the Revolution; The General Theory of Employment, Interest, and Money. By John Maynard Keynes. New York: Harcourt, Brace & World." *The New York Times*, May 16, 1965.

Louise Penny, *Still Life*, St. Martin's Paperbacks, 2005.

Jacquelyn Smith, "12 Tips for Overcoming Your Fear of Change at Work," *Forbes*, January 18, 2013.

Warren Berger, "The Power of 'Why?' and 'What If?'" *The New York Times*, July 2, 2016.

Tom Peters, goodreads.com.

Harry Warner, quoteinvestigator.com.

Rosabeth Moss Kanter, "Ten Reasons People Resist Change," *Harvard Business Review*, September 25, 2012.

Atul Gawande, "Slow Ideas," *The New Yorker*, July 22, 2013.

Chapter Ten

Willy Staley, "Mike Judge, The Bard of Suck," *The New York Times*, April 13, 2017.

Afterword

Tom Peters, Goodreads.com.

A Note About the Academy of Motion Picture Arts and Sciences and the Academy Awards

The mission of the Academy of Motion Picture Arts and Sciences (Academy) is to "recognize and uphold excellence in the motion picture arts and sciences, inspire imagination, and connect the world through the medium of motion pictures." The Academy is a phenomenal organization that makes the movies magical for all of us and preserves the history of the movies and all the remarkable individuals who play a role in making them.

Throughout the book, I refer to "Oscar," "Oscars," "Academy Award," and "Academy Awards." The Academy owns these registered trademarks and service marks.

Whether you live in or visit Los Angeles, there is no better experience than visiting the Academy Museum of Motion Pictures. Its exhibitions, screenings, and programs should not be missed. I encourage you to become a Museum Member, too.

This book is written with nothing but awe, respect, and thanks to those who bring stories to the screen.

ACKNOWLEDGEMENTS

DAVID: First, to everyone that I have cited in the Closing Credits, thank you. I have learned a great deal from each of you, and I know our readers have, too.

I love the IMDb website. It is a treasure trove of movie information. I appreciate all those who produce and contribute to it.

I was excited to serve as the Executive Director of the Motion Picture Industry Pension & Health Plans because I love movies. I have the greatest respect for the thousands of professionals who make them. One of my greatest professional pleasures was serving MPI members and their families.

My good friend and fellow Jayhawk, Robert Prentice, a distinguished professor, scholar, and teacher at the McCombs School of Business at the University of Texas at Austin, added invaluable editing and insight that improved everything about this book. I can't thank him enough. Rock Chalk!

And when I went searching for an illustrator, I had no idea the best of the bunch would be my Denver neighbor,

Elliot Lang. It was a pleasure to work with Elliot, and his illustrations added energy and zip to the text.

Speaking of Denver neighbors, copy editor *extraordinaire* Eric Hübler corrected all my editorial mistakes and improved the final copy.

Tom Howard, a distinguished and experienced intellectual property lawyer, kept a keen eye on the text and provided me with excellent editorial advice.

Finally, my coauthor Tony Picchioni kept me focused when my energy flagged and encouraged me when I was ready to throw in the towel on this project. Little did I know on my first day at work at the Texas Municipal Retirement System in Austin when I saw an appointment with "Dr. Picchioni" on my calendar, that Tony would become one of my closest colleagues and friends.

TONY: No person is an island.

I've had the pleasure of partnering with many cutting-edge teachers and colleagues working to expand leadership training. A special thanks goes to Dr. Robert Patterson, former Dean of SMU's Center of Dispute Resolution and Clinical Counseling, for trusting me to take my novel leadership ideas and then to develop them into a nationally recognized leadership program.

I'm grateful for the opportunity to expand my leadership work into the field of medicine by partnering with James Fleshman, M.D., and Harry Papaconstantinou,

M.D. These two outstanding surgeons are setting a higher standard for medical education because of their belief that today's medical students need training in interpersonal communication and conflict management to be successful.

Elisa Reiter provided many comments that significantly improved the text.

And, of course, this book would still be an idea without my friend and coauthor, David Wescoe. David's passion, skill, and humor take his commitment to engaged leadership to a higher level. This book is a testament not only to our friendship, but to our joint belief that stellar leadership skills can be acquired.

About the Authors

David Wescoe is a former Wall Street lawyer, corporate General Counsel, Chief Financial Officer, CEO, and accomplished public servant. At the San Diego City Employees' Retirement System, David was named Most Admired CEO by Vistage and the *San Diego Business Journal*, and the San Diego City Council proclaimed March 9 David B. Wescoe Day (which is celebrated annually by David's wife and four grown children). During his tenure at the San Diego County Employees Retirement Association, a *San Diego Union-Tribune* profile said, "Wescoe . . . who rehabilitated the operations and reputation of San Diego's municipal pension system [has] amazingly surpassed himself at the county's system. 'The accomplishments are unprecedented,' says one long-time SDCERA board member." And Texas Governor Greg Abbott commissioned David an Honorary Texan for his "visionary leadership" at the Texas Municipal Retirement System.

A native Kansan, David attended Brown University and graduated from the University of Kansas and Columbia Law School. He has served on and chaired numerous nonprofit and educational boards, including serving on the board and as Chair of the University of Kansas Alumni Association and as a Trustee of Trinity School in New York City.

Learn more about David at WescoeConsulting.com.

Anthony Picchioni, PhD, is a distinguished counselor with extensive organizational and change management and coaching experience. He has taught conflict management and coached business executives with Fortune 500 companies around the world. For almost two decades, Tony served as the department chair of the master's programs in Dispute Resolution and Counseling, which he created, at Southern Methodist University in Dallas, Texas. He currently is an educational consultant working in the areas of leadership development and conflict management for the Baylor University Medical Center in Dallas. He is the author of three other books: *Mediation: Skills and Techniques*, *Pessimism to Realistic Hope*, and *Being Complex Without Having A Complex*. Tony graduated from the University of North Texas and completed postdoctoral work at Harvard Law School, the University of Colorado at Boulder, and Pepperdine University.

About the Illustrator

Elliot Lang is an award-winning illustrator who lives in Denver. He has created book covers and interior illustrations, posters for bands and concerts, packaging for food and beverages, and advertisements. He has a passion for the preservation of nature and enjoys all that Colorado's landscapes offer. Elliot is available for speaking opportunities and commissions at elliotlang.com.